The Early All-Stars

ALSO BY BRENT KELLEY

*In the Shadow of the Babe: Interviews with
Baseball Players Who Played With or Against Babe Ruth*
(McFarland, 1995)

*Baseball Stars of the 1950s:
Interviews with All-Stars of the Game's Golden Era*
(McFarland, 1993)

*The Case For:
Those Overlooked by the Baseball Hall of Fame*
(McFarland, 1992)

The Early All-Stars

*Conversations with Standout Baseball
Players of the 1930s and 1940s*

by BRENT KELLEY

McFarland & Company, Inc., Publishers
Jefferson, North Carolina, and London

To Bob and Doug

Front cover photographs (clockwise from top left): Al Zarilla, Ace Adams, Bill Rigney, Mel Harder (all courtesy of *The National Pastime*)

British Library Cataloguing-in-Publication data are available

Library of Congress Cataloguing-in-Publication Data

Kelley, Brent P.
    The early all-stars : conversations with standout baseball players of the 1930s and 1940s / by Brent Kelley.
       p.   cm.
    Includes bibliographical references and index.
    ISBN 0-7864-0204-0 (sewn softcover : 50# alkaline paper) ∞
    1. Baseball players — United States — Interviews. 2. All-Star Baseball Game — History. I. Title.
GV865.A1K445   1997
796.357'092'2 — dc21
[B]   96-40921
                                                               CIP

©1997 Brent Kelley. All rights reserved

No part of this book, specifically including the index, may be reproduced or transmitted in any form or by any means, electronic or mechanical, including photocopying or recording, or by any information storage and retrieval system, without permission in writing from the publisher.

Manufactured in the United States of America

McFarland & Company, Inc., Publishers
   Box 611, Jefferson, North Carolina 28640

Acknowledgments

The 17 former players interviewed herein are to be acknowledged for their kindness and courtesy in allowing me to take time that they could undoubtedly have spent in other ways. I enjoyed each and every interview to the fullest and I'm happy to say that I've made friendships with some fine gentlemen.

These interviews all appeared earlier in *Sports Collectors Digest* in different forms and I want to acknowledge Tom Mortenson and Rick Hines of that publication. The photos are from various sources: George Brace, *The National Pastime*, and several teams: Cincinnati Reds, Cleveland Indians, Detroit Tigers, Pittsburgh Pirates, and San Francisco Giants. Their cooperation is appreciated.

Contents

Acknowledgments	v
Introduction: A Brief History of the All-Star Selection Process	1
ACE ADAMS *His Name Says It All*	3
SAM CHAPMAN *Football Hero*	13
HARLOND CLIFT *Darkie*	23
ELBIE FLETCHER *Gold Glove*	31
MEL HARDER *Art Teacher*	43
SID HUDSON *Second Division*	59
WILLARD MARSHALL *Old Country Boy*	69
JOE MOORE *Team Player*	81
PAT MULLIN *Four Years to the War*	91
ANDY PAFKO *Handy Andy*	102
MEL PARNELL *The Fenway Southpaw*	115
BILL RIGNEY *Full Circle*	129
CONNIE RYAN *A Brave in Three Cities*	145
DICK SISLER *The Whiz Kids' Biggest Hit*	153
BILL VOISELLE *No. 96*	163
BURGESS WHITEHEAD *Gashouse Gang*	173
AL ZARILLA *Fournier's Find*	179
Bibliography	191
Index	193

Introduction: A Brief History of the All-Star Selection Process

The All-Star Game was created in 1933 and until it became a popularity contest in recent years, those selected were indeed deserving of the honor.

The game was the idea of Arch Ward, sports editor of the *Chicago Tribune*, and was intended originally to be a one-time event, played in connection with Chicago's Century of Progress Exposition. Ward received permission from baseball commissioner Kenesaw Mountain Landis to hold the game and it was scheduled for July 6 in Comiskey Park.

And it caught on. It was so well-received that plans were made for it to become an annual event, moving each year to a different Major League city. No game was played in 1945 due to wartime restrictions.

The managers in 1933 were John McGraw for the National League and Connie Mack for the American, but from 1934 on they would be the managers of the previous year's pennant winners (if they were still employed the following year).

Ward thought the players should be chosen by the fans and that's the way it was done the first two years. In 1935 the selection was turned over to the rival managers and in 1938 the squads were picked by the eight managers in each league. The fans regained the voting rights in 1947, but in 1957 the Cincinnati faithful stuffed the ballot boxes, resulting in an overwhelming number of Reds in the starting lineup, so the next year the voting was turned over to the players, managers, and coaches. They could not vote for members of their own team or players in the other league. Then in 1970 the vote was returned to the fans and remains that way today.

The size of the All-Star squads has changed over the years, as well. The original 1933 teams contained 18 men but it increased to 20 the next year, 21 in 1936, 23 in 1937, 25 in 1939, and 28 in 1969 when continued expansion made it difficult to represent each team in the game.

From 1959 through 1962, two All-Star games were played. But when the schedule enlarged to 162 games following expansion it became difficult to allot the break for the second game, so in 1963 it became a one-time affair once more.

Represented in the following pages are All-Stars from the early days of the game, from the '30s through the early '50s. Some played on perennial powerhouses, some played on teams buried in the lower reaches of the standings, but all stood out and all earned a spot in baseball history as All-Stars.

ACE ADAMS

Ace Adams (George Brace photograph).

His Name Says It All
NL All-Star 1943

"The game has changed so much that they're all just showboats and actors."

— Ace Adams

Back in 1912, when Mr. and Mrs. Adams named their new baby boy Ace, they knew what they were doing.

Ace grew up to be an ace.

At a time in baseball history when some managers were beginning to recognize the need for a dependable pitcher in the bullpen, Ace set the pace.

He had been a successful starter in the minors for several years when he joined the New York Giants in 1941 at the rather advanced age (for a rookie) of 29. He became a reliever on Opening Day that season and from then through 1945 set numerous relief records.

The conception today is that all early relievers were placed in that role because they couldn't cut it as starters, but that was not the case with Ace. He made seven major league starts and compiled a 4-2 record, but his greater value out of the bullpen kept him there.

Among Ace's accomplishments:
•Led the NL in Games three times (in a row)
•Led the NL in Games Finished four times (in a row)
•Led the NL in Saves twice (in a row)
•Led the NL in Relief Wins once
•Set six records: Most Games, season (70, 1943); Most Games Relieved, season (67, 1943); Most Games Finished, season (57, 1943); Most Games, No Starts, season (61, 1942); Most Relief Wins plus Saves, season (26, 1945); Most Games Finished, career (218).

Ace jumped to the Mexican League in 1946, lured by an offer of $50,000. Commissioner Happy Chandler banned him (and all of the other jumpers) from playing professional baseball in United States for five years and, although the ban was lifted in 1949, Ace was in his late-thirties and did not return.

Life after baseball has been better to Ace than to most. After all, how many ex-ballplayers have a 500-acre farm just to hunt on?

Tell us about your career.
Ace Adams: I was pitching ball in San Francisco for an industrial league club. I was picked up by a club, signed a little contract, and a bunch of us went to Oklahoma, out there during the dust storms. Bartlesville, Oklahoma. We worked out there and then we were sent out.

They sent me to the Evangeline League in Louisiana in 1935. I won 20 the first year and went back the next year and won 20. I went to Jeanerette in '36, in the same league. I couldn't move so I was just about to quit. I led the league in strikeouts, played the outfield, won 20 games, and couldn't move.

I went home and got a call from the manager I'd had at Jeanerette. He took over Cordele (Georgia) and asked me if I'd come and play. I told him I didn't know — it looked like no matter how many you win you can't move up anywhere. So he talked me into playing for him for a year. I think I got $150 a month. (Laughs) I pitched 30 complete ballgames, won 28, won one in the playoffs.

I had 68 wins in three years, led every league in strikeouts, struck out 218 at Cordele. The next year I moved up to B-ball — Winston-Salem, North Carolina, 1938. The year before, '37, it was the world's worst ballclub. They didn't win anything. I go up there and got to pitching up there and B-ball wasn't any different than anything else.

I had a month to go and Alvin Crowder, played in Washington, owned the ballclub. He called somebody and said, "Somebody better pick up this fella. I've got a hell of a pitcher down here." They said, "He's too small." Made some kinda excuse. I was pitching at 186 (pounds) and was in good shape and all.

Anyway, I had a month to go and I had 17 wins and was leading the league in strikeouts. Alvin Crowder told me, "We're having a night for you. I'll give you a shotgun or the price of a shotgun. You've done a great deal for me, you've filled the stands."

I said, "Give me the money. I ain't got no place to hunt. (Laughs) I'll take the money. Maybe it'll get me through the winter." I wasn't making very much up there, either.

He said, "Nashville wants you. You've been called up. They need a pitcher bad." That was the Southern Association.

I pitched one inning that night at Winston-Salem — had a big crowd there. I went and had to catch the bus over to Knoxville, where I joined Nashville.

Charlie Dressen was managing Nashville then. They tried to sign me for about 200–250 dollars a month. I said, "No. Give me $300 a month or I'm going on down to Florida where my wife is." So I got $300 a month there.

I got there that morning and there was a double-header — Nashville against Knoxville. I had to pitch the second ballgame. I pitched two extra innings and it was tied. They didn't have lights then so it was called on account of darkness, 4-to-4. The first baseman made an error and let in two runs or I had 'em beat, 4-to-2. That's my first game in the Southern Association.

The next season I went in there and did pretty well and got hurt. In 1940 I led the Southern Association in strikeouts, I won 13 and lost 5. That's when I got hurt. I reached out for a line drive and it hit me on my pitching hand — on my wrist — so I couldn't throw a curve ball very easy, couldn't bend my wrist. I pitched about two months there with kind of a dinky curve and a fast ball and change of pace.

I didn't belong to anybody then — just belonged to the Nashville club.

Then I won two games in the Dixie Series against Fort Worth. Ray Starr was pitching for Fort Worth. He pitched a little in the big leagues. I beat 'em, 7-to-3 or 4, in that little cracker box. They said, "Wait'll we get Adams out to Houston and that big ball park and we'll wear him out out there." Hell, I liked to pitch in big ball parks, too. (Laughs)

They didn't even get a man to third base (in Houston). I shut 'em out. So I won two in the Dixie Series.

Larry Gilbert owned the ballclub. He has two sons that played baseball — Tookie and Charlie. Tookie played with us in Nashville, left-handed hitter.

We had one more to win in Houston. I said, "I ain't coming to the ball park." Larry said, "Hell, no. You can stay away." I said, "If you can't win the next one, wait'll we get back to Nashville and I'll close out." I was a little cocky. (Laughs)

But (George) Jeffcoat pitched and won the next night. I wasn't even there. I couldn't stay away — I tried to get in the ballpark and they wouldn't let me in. Didn't recognize me. (Laughs)

We got home and they had a big party for us. When the train got in it was early in the morning. Most everybody on the train was inebriated — they all had plenty to drink and they were sleeping. (Laughs) The train only stopped there for about 30 minutes and then would pull out.

So I was running up and down the train waking everybody up. "Get your butts up! We're in Nashville! We're home!" They were groggy-eyed and everything. I had already been up and dressed and was ready to get home.

Before we got off they had us line up on the steps of the train and they took pictures. There was a big crowd there all around the train. I think I've still got that picture of five or six of us standing on the steps in the door.

My wife was pretty close there and she was waving this headline in the *Nashville Banner*. It said, "Adams Bought by New York Giants." Several more of 'em were waving that and I didn't even know it.

I got with her and we went home and they had a big supper for us downtown that night. I was kinda tired and I just wanted to relax. I said, "I don't think I'll even go to the thing."

She said, "Oh, you got to go! They're kinda counting on you."

So she and I went down there. It was a good thing I went. Larry had a thousand dollar bill for me. I think they sold me for $65,000 and he gave me $1,000. (Laughs)

I go to spring training — we trained in the Orange Bowl but we stayed at the Miami Hilton in Coral Gables. They tried to sign me up for $2,500. "$2,500!" I said. "My God Almighty, I can't live on that!"

They owned you. You were like a mule, you know. I said, "Well, I just don't know. I guess I'll just have to go home again. I just can't live on that. I've got a farm — I can go work it and make more than $500 a month."

So they gave me $3,500. (Laughs) Isn't that something? Living in New York on $3,500.

I had a good spring training. I was really in tip-top shape. I did what

Ace Adams (courtesy of *The National Pastime*).

they wanted me to do. I doubt I was scored on all spring. They didn't let me pitch enough — I needed a *lot* of work.

We got up there in New York, playing Brooklyn on Opening Day. I was up on the bench. They figured me as a relief pitcher. That was 1941, we opened in Brooklyn. I was enjoying the ballgame — first major league ballgame I'd ever seen.

Bill Terry was managing. He said, "Adams, go down in the bullpen and warm up." That was about the fourth or fifth inning. (Carl) Hubbell or (Hal) Schumacher opened — I don't remember which.

I went down there and I was just messing around. Melton was down there—big ol' Cliff Melton. He and I were buddies in spring training. He was 6-feet-5 and I was 5-feet-10½. He kinda took me under his wing and helped me a lot and told me all kinda stuff. *Very* good friend of mine. Every time we went anywhere, he'd say, "Here comes the long and the short of it." (Laughs) We had a good time.

He said, "Ace, I know Bill Terry. You'd better warm up. Now get ready, 'cause your butt's going in that ballgame."

I said, "Noooo, he'll never put me in this Opening Day thing."

He said, "Do this for me: Get hot like you were gonna start." He knew Bill Terry better'n I did.

First thing I knew, we got in trouble and I really got hot—warmed up real good. I was ready to go. So damned if he didn't call me in and put me right in that ballgame—first major league ballgame I'd ever seen. I pitched the last four innings. I think the score was tied when I went in and I held 'em for four innings and we scored a run and I got credit for the win. First major league ballgame I'd ever seen.

Terry come running out there. I belonged to Brooklyn at one time and Terry had to show 'em up a little bit. You know, he said one time, "Is Brooklyn still in the league?" That caused all this rivalry all these years.

He picked me up in his arms and the whole ballclub come around me. We got in the clubhouse and (Eddie) Brannick was our traveling secretary. Terry says, "Where's Brannick? Tell Brannick to come in here!"

Brannick came in, right before the whole ballclub in the clubhouse. "What do you want?"

He said, "Tear up Adams's contract right as of now and add a $1,000 to his contract! Starting today!" Right in front of the whole damn ballclub. So that's the way I started.

Did you like being switched from starting to relieving?

No. I told 'em it didn't make any difference to me—I wanted some money.

I kept pitching in relief and said, "Listen. I can start." Starting pitchers were all making more money than I was. I said, "I can start and I can finish. I'm in good shape."

I think it was 1943, I was in nine out of the first 11 ballgames. When we came back, nobody was in shape but me. I said, "I want to start 'cause I want to make some money." You couldn't make any money relieving. Relieving was low on the totem pole.

Mel Ott was managing then. He said, "All right. We'll schedule you to start. We have a double-header with Boston on Sunday and you and Cliff can pitch the double-header. You can pitch the second game." That was all put in the paper and everything.

On Thursday I pitched two innings in relief. Friday I didn't pitch but I was up in the bullpen. Saturday I pitched four innings and won that ballgame against the Braves. Trying to keep me from starting is what they were doing.

Mel said, "Don't look like you can start tomorrow."

I said, "Listen, Mel, you're just trying to screw me up. I'll tell you something: I'm gonna start that damn ballgame if I don't pitch but three innings! I'm scheduled to start it — you've had it in the paper."

"All right, hard head. You're gonna start it." I know damn well he was pulling against me — didn't want me to pitch well.

After the four innings on Saturday, I turned right around and pitched nine innings on Sunday — had a no-hitter going into the ninth. (Laughs) I beat 'em, I think, 7–to–2 or something like that. They scored a couple of runs off me in the ninth. I still have the clipping.

They called me in the office the next day. They said, "We can't afford to use you as a starter 'cause we can't use you enough. You can pitch every day. Will you relieve the rest of the season if we double your salary?"

I said, "Sure will. And I'll come out and help the groundskeeper." (Laughs) That made me happy as hell so I continued to relieve.

I pitched quite a few ballgames — broke the record twice for number of games.

You were chosen for the 1943 All-Star Game but didn't pitch.

No. Got to watch, though. (Laughs)

You jumped to the Mexican League in 1946. Why?

I just made 50,000 bucks. I was only making $9,000 — that was my top salary. They wanted me down there so I went for $50,000 — can't blame me for that.

I was gonna retire after the year anyhow — can't make over $9,000. I had an established farm down here. They offered me a good contract to come back after they found out (about the jump).

After I played in Mexico, I was managing a little ol' team down here for the Dixie Lilly Milling Company in Florida and they were paying me good money. If we won, we were gonna to go to the thing in Wichita, Kansas. That was about '47.

They called the minor league big shots and they barred me off of the field, said I was barred from baseball. I had it won all but one more game and I was gonna pitch it and I figured I was gonna win that.

That was carrying it too far. I loved baseball and all, but when they barred me off semi-pro — not even pro — that's too far. That knocked me out of money so I got me a lawyer — a country lawyer right here in Albany and he contacted a big firm and they handled my case. We settled out of court before it went very far. It's a shame they had to do that.

Who was the best hitter you saw?

(Stan) Musial was a great hitter and ol' Johnny Mize was a long ball hitter. He came over and played first base with the Giants.

Somebody asked who was the toughest hitter I ever faced and I said, "All of 'em. They're all tough."

One guy hit me pretty good — Nick Etten, left-handed hitter played with Philadelphia — first base. He could hit me pretty damn good. Good player.

Who was the best pitcher you saw?

I saw so many of 'em. Of course, he was going out, but Carl Hubbell was the greatest. That screwball of his — any new man that come up, you guaranteed he was gonna strike out twice. That thing just come up there and fell off.

(Kirby) Higbe was pretty good, but he didn't last long. And Bucky Walters converted from a third baseman to a pitcher. Didn't have a hell of a fast ball but he was just a hell of a pitcher.

You missed the pension plan by one year.

Yeah, I missed it, but I'm doing good without it.

I have a lot to do. I have farms and I have great hunting on my farms. I have one 500-acre farm just 30 minutes from my house. I have worlds of deer and a 100-ton peanut allotment on my three farms. I plant a lot of stuff for the deer and I have wild turkey, quails, doves, and everything.

I go out and check on my store. I got a liquor store and two restaurants just a little way from the house here, so I don't exactly need the pension.

My son runs the liquor store — does a little over two million (dollars) a year. He rents the building from me and he's got a seafood and oyster bar right on the same lot there. I've got the whole corner — I bought it in 1948. He's doing $800,000 in the restaurant. (Laughs) It's the most popular place in town.

I've got another restaurant behind there. It's a different type of restaurant — they don't conflict with each other. One of 'em sells vegetable-type stuff and it's closed when he does all his big business. His is more or less a night club.

I go out to the store and fool around there or I go hunting down on the farm. I get kinda lonesome — I lost my wife a while back. We'd been married 53½ years.

I've got a garden down on the farm. Nobody lives on it. I put out a hundred quail. It's really a hunting place; that's all I bought it for.

We're down here below the gnat line. Those gnats really bother me. A Yankee drove down here and went home and said, "Those Georgia people are the friendliest people in the world. They sit on their porches and just wave at you all day." (Laughs) They're sitting there fanning gnats.

A Yankee was down here and the station man was filling his car at one of these little country service stations and he was standing there fanning the gnats. He said, "Damn! These little flies are awful! When they grow up, they're gonna really be something!" (Laughs)

Do you receive much fan mail?

Oh, my God, yeah! I get all kinds of letters—five or six every week. They send me everything to sign.

I got one the other day from a fellow out in San Clemente, California. He said he used to lean over the wall there in the Polo Grounds in right-center field and watch me warm up with Ray Berres, the bullpen catcher. He said he remembered how that ball used to pop in that glove when I was warming up. He said how he hated the Dodgers and now he said he works for 'em. He sent me something to sign and asked me to write something to him. He sent a stamped envelope—they all send stamped envelopes.

One guy sent me four baseballs to autograph. It cost him six or seven dollars to send 'em each way.

Do you enjoy hearing from the fans?

Oh, yeah. I enjoy it. I answer every letter. Sometimes they want all kinds of stuff—too much. With those, I'll just autograph one thing and send it back. One guy wanted one of my canceled checks, even.

Would you be a ballplayer today?

No, not the way it is now. The game has changed *so* much that they're all just showboats now and actors. There's not a one of 'em can bunt. They don't even practice bunting. They're all just swinging from their ass, trying to hit home run, home run, home run.

They don't play like a team like we used to. Pitchers can't even bunt anymore. It's a different game and the fans don't know the difference. We played together and we tried to get that run or two 'cause if you got a run or two that pitcher was gonna hold 'em.

There are guys hitting .198 drawing a million to two million dollars. They get that kind of money, they don't care what they do. They got it made. It's ruined it.

All we had to draw from was the gate receipts, but now the TV is there. I don't blame 'em for getting all that money because TV pays so much. But I'll tell you something: It's gonna revert back. This thing's gonna change. There's gonna be a hell of a lot of free agents here pretty soon. You just watch and see.

Of course, we never had a chance to be a free agent. We either played and took what they offered or we went home—we couldn't play for anybody else. They owned you like a mule.

If you went back fifty or sixty years, would you play again?

Oh, hell, yeah! I sure would.

* * *

Here is a look at the records for pitching appearances without a start in a season, beginning with the first person to have over 50.

Year	Pitcher, team	G
1925	Fred Marberry, Washington	55
1942	ACE ADAMS, New York (NL)	61
1950	Jim Konstanty, Philadelphia (NL)	74
1964	John Wyatt, Kansas City	81
1965	Ted Abernathy, Chicago (NL)	84
1969	Wayne Granger, Cincinnati	90
1973	Mike Marshall, Montreal	92
1974	Mike Marshall, Los Angeles	106

ACE TOWNSEND ADAMS
Born March 2, 1912, Willows, CA
Ht. 5'10½"   Wt. 182   Batted and Threw Right

Year	Team	G	IP	W	L	PCT	H	BB	SO	SHO	SV	ERA
1941	NYN	38	71	4	1	.800	84	35	18	0	1	4.82
1942		61*	88	7	4	.636	69	31	33	0	11	1.84
1943		70*	140.1	11	7	.611	121	55	46	0	9	2.82
1944		65*	137.2	8	11	.421	149	58	32	0	13*	4.25
1945		65	113	11	9	.550	109	44	35	0	15*	3.42
1946		3	2.2	0	1	.000	9	1	3	0	0	16.88
6 years		302	551.5	41	33	.554	541	224	171	0	49	3.47

*Led league

All-Star Game

| 1943 | National | Selected, did not play |

SAM CHAPMAN

Sam Chapman (George Brace photograph).

Football Hero
AL All-Star 1946

"I was a lost soul."
— Sam Chapman

January 1, 1938, Pasadena, California. The University of California's Golden Bears were in their first Rose Bowl since 1929; their opponent was Alabama's mighty Crimson Tide. These were the days before the Big 10 champ was an automatic Rose Bowl participant and Alabama had made the trip west four previous times with their worst outcome having been a tie. Three years previously they had demolished a strong Stanford team.

Leading Cal was their unanimous All-American halfback, Sam Chapman. 'Bama coach Frank Thomas knew this and keyed his defense to stop Sam's ground game. As a result, Sam was held to only 12 carries for 65 yards (5.4 avg.). Cal adjusted but 'Bama didn't; Vic Bottari, the Bears' other halfback, was given the ball 32 times and he picked up 146 yards (4.6 avg.) and scored two TD's. The final score: Cal 13, Alabama 0.

Sam's contributions were not limited to running though. He kicked the extra point and when the Tide was able to stop the Bears' offense, his punts put them deep in their own territory. In fact, it was one of his punts that 'Bama fumbled (one of four fumbles for the day) which set up one of the touchdowns.

Sam also played baseball for UC. Ty Cobb saw him playing and recommended to his old employer, Connie Mack, that he sign him for the Philadelphia Athletics. And so he did. An early bonus baby, Mr. Mack gave Sam $6,000 and a major league contract to sign. By today's standards $6,000 is pocket change to a ballplayer, but in 1938 the country was still recovering from the Great Depression and there was considerable unrest in Europe. Six thousand dollars was a king's ransom.

Sam joined the A's in Cleveland on May 16, 1938, as soon as he could get there after finishing school, and stayed with them as a regular through 1950 (with four years out for the war).

Along the way there were many milestones. On May 5, 1939, against the Browns, Sam hit for the cycle as the A's downed St. Louis, 10–5. (It was a good day for the entire Philadelphia outfield: Bob Johnson, Dee Miles, and Sam had ten hits and eight RBI's between them.)

The next day Sam homered in his first two trips to the plate, although St. Louis won that one, 7–5.

A few years later, on August 15, 1946, Sam hit three homers (and a single) against the Red Sox and drove in four of the A's runs in a 5–3 defeat of Boston. Philadelphia had only three other hits on the day.

Sam eventually played in three no-hitters and had an important role in all three.

The first was on July 10, 1947. Cleveland's Don Black, a former teammate of Sam in Philadelphia, shut down the A's, 3–0 although he walked six. Black was making a comeback after almost drinking himself out of the game. He had joined Alcoholics Anonymous the previous winter and was a new man. There were a couple of fine plays behind him, notably a 400-foot fly hit by Hank Majeski that center fielder George Metkovich broke in on but recovered and ran down. But the toughest part of the game for Black was a 45-minute rain delay.

The final out was a vicious shot back to the mound by Sam that Black just happened to get his glove in front of, otherwise it was through to center field. The throw to first easily retired Sam and Black had pitched the first no-hitter in Municipal Stadium history in front of the largest crowd (47,871) to ever witness a no-hitter to that point. (The reason for the large crowd: They were anticipating seeing Larry Doby, just signed, become the first black player in American League history. They were disappointed.)

(Toward the end of the next season, Black collapsed on the field from a brain hemorrhage, lived, but never played again.)

The losing pitcher to Black was A's rookie right-hander Bill McCahan, who also played in the old National Basketball League. Eight weeks later, September 3, 1947, McCahan was on the other end of a no-hitter. He downed the Senators, 3–0, in a near-perfect game; the only base runner reached on an error by first baseman Ferris Fain, ironically one of the finest defensive first sackers in the history of the game. He had fielded Stan Spence's hard grounder and hurried his throw to the covering McCahan.

In this game, Sam made three excellent catches in center field to take away hits and drove in the first run of the game in the second inning.

(Mack forbade McCahan, 10–5 in 1947, from playing basketball after that season so Bill got an off-season job that year loading and unloading oil drums and hurt his arm. He was only 5–8 over the next two seasons and then was gone from the majors.)

The next no-hit game for Sam was on July 1, 1951. He was an Indian at this point, having been traded to Cleveland on May 10 for two players, and it was Bob Feller's third and last no-hitter. Errors by Feller and shortstop Ray Boone had allowed the Tigers to score a run and entering the bottom of the eighth the score was tied, 1–1. With one out, Sam tripled (the only extra-base hit of the game) and rookie Milt Nielsen (or Nielson, depending on your reference) came in to run for him. One out later, Luke Easter singled him home; it was Nielsen's only run of the season.

(Feller had not been sharp that day. In the third inning, pitching coach Mel Harder had gone to the mound to see if he wanted to come out. Feller said he'd be okay.)

That was Sam's last season in the majors. He was in the Pacific Coast League briefly before leaving baseball, but he enjoyed every minute of it while he was there.

After a college career as an All-American football player, was professional football a temptation?

Sam Chapman: Yeah, it was, but I had already started playing baseball. I went directly to the A's from school. I missed maybe a month (of the season). I finished my exams and left.

I took a train back to Cleveland and met Connie Mack and played the first day and from then on. Mr. Mack needed players at the time.

Who scouted you for the A's?

It was Ty Cobb. I'd never met Ty Cobb till after I started playing for Connie Mack but he recommended me and I don't know if he *ever* saw me play.

You received a bonus.

They gave me $6,000 and a $2,500 salary. I was rich. (Laughs) I was offered more by the Yankees, but I signed with the A's because of Cobb.

Whose spot did you take when you joined the A's?

I don't remember. They were kind of short on outfielders. I was an infielder when I left here. I played shortstop in college and when I arrived there, Mr. Mack says, "You're playing center field today." So that was it. (Laughs)

Who was the shortstop?

Oh, gosh. They were coming and going in those days. I don't know if (Wayne) Ambler was there when I arrived but he was there during my tour.

How was the adjustment to the outfield? That's a tough time to switch positions.

Yeah, but they had Wally Moses and Bob Johnson in right and left field and they both helped me very much.

I had thought that you were always an outfielder. You had excellent range and led the league in total chances per game several times.

Well, out pitching wasn't too good. (Laughs)

So you're saying they gave you plenty of opportunities. The A's really did need pitching badly when you were there. Was that all that was necessary to have a better team?

Yes, we'd have been a much better team. You know, they carried, I think, 11 pitchers in those days — I guess they still do — and we usually had eight or nine. Mr. Mack was broke, I guess.

That was pretty much a hand-to-mouth operation for many years.

Yeah. It was for some time. He didn't get the players and whether he was completely broke or what, I don't know.

The outfield was outstanding: you, Moses, and Johnson.

They were good outfielders, good hitters.

Does Bob Johnson belong in the Hall of Fame?

I would think so. Let's see, I went in the service after the '41 season and Bob was gone when I came back. He was a big, strong guy and he was a very good hitter and a good outfielder.

So was Moses — a very good outfielder and a good hitter.

Sam Chapman (courtesy of *The National Pastime*).

You enlisted and spent four years as a Navy pilot. Did you play ball in the service?

Very little. I played when I was in flight training, which made me unhappy. It interfered with my flight training and cost me a couple of months to finish. You know the All-Star Game they play every year? Well, they had a second one with several of the fellows who were in the service, so I got stuck with that thing.

Did you see much action in the war?

No action. I spent four years and I instructed for two years, then spent the rest of the time up and down the (West) Coast waiting for the invasion of Japan. We had some new fighter planes that were designed small and fast just for that thing and we never used them.

You rejoined the A's late in the 1945 season.

I was just a few months under the age limit when I got into flying, so I was one of the first that they let go. I had gotten a letter from Connie Mack asking if I could come back for a couple of weeks. I really didn't want to get out but I had just gotten married and my wife wanted to get out.

Those four years in the service cost you some big years.

I just really got started in pro baseball and my first two years weren't too good and then I had a good year and I went in the service.

You weren't chosen for the All-Star Game in 1941 when you had an outstanding year but were in '46 when your number weren't as good.

I think it was just because I had that good year before I went in the service.

In 1951, after being most of the A's offense for many years, you were traded to the Indians. How did you feel about that?

I didn't like it much except Cleveland had a chance to go to the World Series and they needed another outfielder, so they traded me for a couple of players.

That was the first real pennant contender you'd been on.

Yeah, it was nice.

Is there one game that stands out?

I can think of one that stands out and that was my first game I played. (Laughs) I was a lost soul. I was in center field and I had never worn sunglasses. There was a high fly to center, which I could catch easily normally, and it was in the sun and I put the glasses up and put 'em down, put 'em up, and then threw 'em away and almost got hit in the head. (Laughs)

Then I picked up the ball and threw it into the stands over third base, where the hitter was running. That was my start. (Laughs)

What did you do at the plate?

I don't know whether I got a hit or not, but a big pitcher was pitching for Cleveland and the first pitch he threw I hit a line drive and hit him on the shin. He was kind of an ornery guy and for the years he played I'd be knocked down a couple of times every time I came to bat. It was Johnny Allen. (Laughs)

(Sam went 0–for–4 with an RBI.)

Speaking of pitchers, who was the best you saw?

Probably all-around would be Bob Feller.

The war really cost him.

It cost a lot of fellows a lot.

Who was the toughest on you?

There was a little guy pitching on the Detroit team and I had a *hell* of a time getting a hit off of him. Tommy Bridges. He had a sneaky fastball.

Who was the best player?

Two of 'em, I would say. Joe DiMaggio was the best all-around player and Ted Williams was the best hitter.

With the pitching staff there in Philadelphia, you got to see them at their best.

(Laughs) Yeah.

Ted Williams, when he broke .400, was at Philadelphia—1941. They finished up the season at Philadelphia and he was hitting .400. It was a double-header and they wanted to take him out of the first game and he wouldn't do it and he played the second game and added a few more points to it.

How much fan mail do you receive today?

I probably get three or four letters a week—sometimes more, sometimes less. They're autograph requests. I sign. A lot of people charge for 'em but I don't.

Do you have any regrets from your baseball career?

No, I can't say that I do. I enjoyed every minute of it and I enjoyed going into the service, not that I wanted to at the time.

Would you go back and do it again?

Yeah, I think so.

Would you try football?

Maybe, but not both of 'em. When I first got back to Philadelphia—the first year or the second year—I had been drafted by Washington (Redskins) for football and Detroit traded for me to play football and baseball in Detroit. Thank God, Mr. Mack wouldn't let me go 'cause those days you played 60 minutes—defense and offense. (Laughs)

* * *

Sam's right when he says the war cost a lot of fellows a lot. How much, of course, is open to conjecture, but let's try to see what it may have cost Sam in the way of baseball stats.

Sam was in the Navy from 1942 to 1945. He was 26 when he went in so these were four peak years as far as baseball production goes and we can't guess at how good he may have been during the time but let's assume that, for those four years, he performed at the same level as he had the four nearest years to his missed time—that is, the two full years just prior to entering service and the two full years immediately after returning. Some of you may disagree, but this is probably the minimum level at which he would have performed.

For those years then, 1940, '41, '46, and '47, Sam had 82 home runs, 341 runs, 321 RBI's, and a .273 BA. Add these to his career totals and this is what we come up with:

262 HR's   1,095 Runs   1,094 RBI's   .270

But that's what might have been. Let's look at fielding and see what actually was.

The careers of Joe and Dominic DiMaggio and Sam make them contemporaries. Joe came up on '36, Sam in '38, and Dom in '40. Joe and Dom each lost three years to the war, Sam four. Joe and Sam left the majors after 1951, Dom after '52 (we're not counting three pinch hit appearances in 1953). Joe had 13 years, Sam and Dom 10 (we're also ignoring the nine games Sam played at the end of '45).

Range is probably the best measure of fielding ability—you can't make the play if you can't get to the ball—so let's look at the ranges of these three in the years in which at least two of them were *regular* outfielders. See the first table below.

Table at the bottom of this page shows us a few other fielding comparisons.

A lot of people will tell you that Dominic was the greatest outfielder the game has ever seen. Many others will tell you Joe was. If either group is correct, where does that put Sam?

TOTAL CHANCES/GAME OF SAM CHAPMAN AND JOE AND DOMINIC DIMAGGIO IN YEARS IN WHICH AT LEAST TWO OF THEM WERE REGULAR OUTFIELDERS

Year	Sam	Joe	Dom	
1938	2.2	2.8	–	(3.1 led)
1939	3.2*	3.0	–	
1940	2.91	2.86	2.78	(3.1 led)
1941	3.2*	2.95	2.90	
1942	service	2.8	3.1*	
1943–45		service		
1946	2.7	2.6	2.9	(3.0 led)
1947	3.1	2.3	3.3*	
1948	3.2	3.0	3.4*	
1949	3.06	2.6	3.07*	
1950	3.2*	2.7	2.8	
1951	**	2.7	2.8	(3.5 led)

*Led league   **Not a regular

THE SAME THREE IN NUMBER OF TIMES LED LEAGUE IN FIELDING DEPARTMENTS

Dept.	Sam	Joe	Dom
PO	4	1*	2**
A	1	1*	3**
E	3	1*	2
DP	1	1	1

Dept.	Sam	Joe	Dom
TC/G	3	0	4**
FA	0	1	0

*Each was before Dom or Sam was in majors
**One of each came in 1942 when Sam was in Navy

SAMUEL BLAKE CHAPMAN
Born April 11, 1916, Tiburon, CA
Ht. 6'   Wt. 185   Batted and Threw Right

Year	Team	G	AB	R	H	2B	3B	HR	RBI	SB	BA	SA
1938	PhiA	114	406	60	105	17	7	17	63	3	.259	.461
1939		140	498	74	134	24	6	15	64	11	.269	.432
1940		134	508	88	140	26	3	23	75	2	.276	.474
1941		143	552	97	178	29	9	25	106	6	.322	.543
1945		9	30	3	6	2	0	0	1	0	.200	.267
1946		146	545	77	142	22	5	20	67	1	.261	.429
1947		149	551	84	139	18	5	14	83	3	.252	.379
1948		123	445	58	115	18	6	13	70	6	.258	.413
1949		154	589	89	164	24	4	24	108	3	.278	.455
1950		140	553	93	139	20	6	23	95	3	.251	.434
1951	PhiA	18	65	7	11	1	0	0	5	0	.169	.185
	CleA	94	246	24	56	9	1	6	36	3	.228	.346
	Year	112	311	31	67	10	1	6	41	3	.215	.312
11 years		1368	4988	754	1329	210	52	180	773	41	.266	.438

All-Star Game

Year	League	G	AB	R	H	2B	3B	HR	RBI	SB	BA	SA
1946	American	1	2	0	0	0	0	0	0	0	.000	.000

HARLOND CLIFT

Harlond Clift (courtesy of Harlond Clift).

Darkie
AL All-Star 1937

"*I always liked kids. That's all the ballplayers are.*"
— Harlond Clift

Third base today is known as a power position, and with good reason. Since 1950, over 60 hot-sackers have hit 20 or more home runs in one or more seasons.

But this is not the way it's always been. In the decade of the 1940s, only eight third basemen hit 20 or more homers in a season and in the '30s, only five, one an outfielder playing out of position, could reach the 20 level.

The first third baseman to reach 20 was Freddy Lindstrom of the Giants. He hit 22 in 1930 but for his career averaged fewer than seven a season, so power was not his forte. Five years later the second 20-homer season at the hot corner was achieved when Pinky Higgins of the A's hit 23.

But the next year, 1936, marked the first of four years Harlond "Darkie" Clift was to hit 20 or more home runs. He had an even 20 that year, then in 1937 he set a record for third basemen with 29, only to break it the next season with 34. Still, power at third was the exception. The first year to see more than one man reach 20 was 1938; in addition to Clift's 34, rookie Ken Keltner of the Indians blasted 26 and veteran Mel Ott of the Giants hit 27 of his National League–leading 36 while playing third.

Clift dropped to 15 in 1939, but that was more than any other third baseman had that year, then he came back with 20 in 1940 and 17 in '41. His single-season high of 34 remained the record for his position (Mel Ott was really an outfielder) until Al Rosen hit 37 in 1950. Table at top of page 29 shows the single-season home run record progression for third basemen. Harlond's other home run records for his position, career (178) and most seasons, 20 or more (4), were also broken in time. Rosen equalled the four seasons of 20-plus just before Eddie Mathews made the record seem inconsequential. Clift's career record stood for 21 years, but Mathews also passed it without blinking.

Harlond joined the St. Louis Browns in 1934 after two solid years with San Antonio in the Texas League. Very little good could be said of the Browns of the '30s. The hitting was not much, but the pitching was horrible. Third base for the Brownies in 1933 had yielded three home runs, 38 RBI's, and a batting average of .205, so there was no hard act for the 21-year-old rookie to follow. As in the minors, he came through with solid numbers, leading the team with 14 homers and driving in 56 runs.

For the next ten years, Clift was the hub of the Browns' offense. He had intermittent help over the years, but he remained from 1934 until illness forced him from the lineup in 1943 the sole bright spot in an otherwise gloomy batting order.

Injury and illness drastically reduced his effectiveness and the Browns traded him to the Senators late in 1943. Limited to only 12 games in 1944, he bounced back in '45 to lead the Senators in home runs with eight (that doesn't sound like many, but remember, it was a par five to the left field fence in old Griffith Stadium).

For the nine full years before his health reduced his effectiveness, however, he averaged 19 home runs, 83 RBI's, 108 runs, and 104 bases on balls. His batting average for that period was .280 and twice, 1936 and '37, he batted over .300. In 1936 he scored 145 runs, the all-time mark for both the Browns and all third basemen, and six other years he scored in excess of 100. Twice he drove in 118 runs, the third highest total ever attained by a Brownie. Also, his 34 homers in 1938 was the second-best total ever for the team and the most by a right-handed batter. Six times he walked more than 100 times, leading the majors in 1939 with 111. Four times he was the team leader in homers, twice in RBI's, and seven times in runs scored.

But Clift was not just an offensive threat. He was the premier defensive third baseman of his time, twice leading the league in fielding and assists and three times in putouts. In 1937 he set the major league records for assists in a season, 405; total chances accepted, 603; total chances, 637; and double plays, 50. None of these records were broken until the season was expanded from 154 games to 162.

Table on page 29 shows the batting and fielding records held by Clift at the time of his retirement and when (or if) they were broken.

The Browns Fan Club acknowledged Harlond's contributions a few years ago, electing him to the Browns Hall of Fame, but hope for greater recognition today for him is probably a dream. He wasn't fully appreciated while he was playing and that seems to have carried over into his retirement. Never considered a Hall of Fame candidate during his eligible years, he is hardly remembered now. But during his prime he could do it all.

Back in the '50s you were a coach with the San Francisco Seals. I believe that was your last job in baseball. Why did you leave the game?

Harlond Clift: The Seals. That was a long time ago. My dad had a cattle ranch here in Washington. His health was failing and he needed help. Nineteen fifty-three was my last year with the Seals.

In '52 or '53, after a Seals game, I went to the dressing room door to try to get some autographs. I was 11 or 12 and the attendant at the door told me to get lost. Just then you walked by and said, "Let the kid in." That was one of the highlights of my life to that point.

You know, I think I remember that. I always liked kids. That's all the ballplayers are. And everyone should be allowed to get autographs.

It's been so long since I was with the Seals. I remember a few of the guys: Reno Cheso, third base; Jim Moran, second. (George) Vico was there for a while. And Walt Judnich; he'd played with me with the Browns. You know, the Seals weren't someone's farm team. Those guys were owned by the club. Some of 'em never made the majors for that reason.

Tommy Heath was the manager. What a great guy. I haven't thought of him in years. He played with me, too. I guess he's gone now. Do you remember anyone else on those teams?

Oh, sure. Elmer Singleton, Johnny McCall, Nini Tornay, Lou Stringer, Al Lyons, Al Lien, Sal Taormina. Leo Hughes was the trainer.

Oh, those names bring back memories. Leo Hughes.

How did you get your nickname, Darkie?

When I went to my first spring training with the Browns, the guys thought my name was "Harlem" instead of "Harlond." Actually Darkie was the best they called me. Back then, before the color line was broken, they could get pretty rough with names. "Blackie" was another, not too bad, but they also called me "Nig" and "Nigger" and lots of other things. It never bothered me. I was just glad to be playing, but my mother came to visit me in St. Louis once and she heard the names and didn't understand at all.

How bad were the Browns when you were there?

Oh, we had a pretty good team usually. Hitting, I mean. But the pitching, oh, it was awful! Just awful! And nobody ever saw us play. We barely averaged a thousand people a day one year.

You had some pretty decent teammates off and on. You played alongside Vern Stephens for a while.

He was a great ballplayer. I taught him how to hit. When he came to us he stood with his feet together; I told him to move 'em apart.

Alcohol ruined his career. I remember once on a train ride he was sick, throwing up over the railing holding a bottle in one hand. He'd puke and then take a swig. I was afraid he'd fall. I tried to get the bottle away from him.

Alcohol and women. He was a real good-lookin' guy — he looked like Superman, like the guy who plays him; you know, Reeve. The women loved him and he loved them. He was married but you'd never know it.

He was the best power hitting shortstop of his time. Does he belong in the Hall of Fame?

That's hard to say. Why not?

Another teammate of yours was Bobo Newsom.

The greatest guy I ever knew! I liked him real well. When he played on your team he was the best friend you ever had, but when he was with the other team he'd stick the ball right in your ribs. What a character! He showed up one spring training with "Bobo Newsom — the Greatest" in lights on the side of his car. He was a big man. Must've been 6–3 or 4 and 220 or so and his wife was a little bitty woman, maybe 4–10. What a pair!

Does he belong in the Hall of Fame?

I'd say yes, what with the guys they're letting in these days.

You held several fielding records for third basemen.

I was fast, quick. I reacted well. I played third like Pepper Martin — knocked the ball down with my chest or whatever. Threw 'em out. Guys like

Harlond Clift (George Brace photograph).

Dimaj (Joe DiMaggio) and Jimmie Foxx would hit shots out of this world down the line. After some games I was one big bruise, but gimme a sandwich and a bottle of beer and I was ready to go again.

With all your great hitting and fielding, you were only chosen for one All-Star Game. Should you have been selected to others?

Probably. Foxx was usually the All-Star third baseman, but he rarely played third in the season. The game I was picked for I didn't play in. Years later, Joe McCarthy, the manager that year, saw me at an old-timers game. He apologized for not playing me — he said he thought I'd make it to another one.

Jimmie Foxx was great, though. He was so strong! He was probably my best friend in the game. He was with me when I met my wife. He died in a bad way — choked. Caught a piece of meat in his throat. A real shock.

DiMaggio was great, too. He had to be the best all-round.

You became ill in 1943 and your career was shortened.

I got mumps. I was too old to get them and they descended. I was really sick. Then I got bursitis in my left shoulder. Thrown from a horse and landed on it. It hurt so bad I couldn't lift my arm; I had to lift my left arm with my right hand to catch the ball. It still bothers me.

What kind of money did you make?

Nothing compared to today. My tops with St. Louis was $13,000. I got $15,000 from Washington.

Do you belong in the Hall of Fame?

That's up to my peers. I can't say.

You know, several years ago I was asked to sign a petition for Ken Keltner for the Hall of Fame. I don't know if he belongs, but I signed it. He was a good player.

* * *

During the peak years of Harlond Clift's career, Jimmie Foxx was usually the AL's starting All-Star third baseman. These were primarily the years when the players were selected by each league's manager. Here are the number of *regular season* games which Foxx actually played at third base in those years.

1935: 2
1936: 1
1937: 0
1938: 0

Yet he was his league's starter at the position in All-Star competition.

SINGLE SEASON HOME RUN RECORD FOR THIRD BASEMEN

	Year	HR
Fred Lindstrom	1930	22
Pinky Higgins	1935	23
HARLOND CLIFT	1937	29
HARLOND CLIFT	1938	34
Al Rosen	1950	37
Eddie Mathews	1953	47
Mike Schmidt	1980	48

RECORDS HELD BY HARLOND CLIFT AT HIS RETIREMENT

Major League Records		Year Set	Year Broken
Most assists, season, 3B	405	1937	1971
Most double plays, season, 3B	50	1937	1971
Most TC accepted, season, 3B	603	1937	
Most home runs, season, 3B	34	1938	1950
Most home runs, career, 3B	178	1945	1956
Most runs, season, 3B	145	1936	
Most seasons, 20+ HR, 3B	4	1940	1956
American League Records			
Most TC, season, 3B	637	1937	
Most double plays, career, 3B	307	1945	1962

HARLOND BENTON (DARKIE) CLIFT

Born August 12, 1912, El Reno, OK, Died April 27, 1992, Yakima, WA
Ht. 5'11"   Wt. 180   Batted and Threw Right

Year	Team	G	AB	R	H	2B	3B	HR	RBI	SB	BA	SA
1934	StLA	147	572	104	149	30	10	14	56	7	.260	.421
1935		137	475	101	140	26	4	11	69	0	.295	.436

Year	Team	G	AB	R	H	2B	3B	HR	RBI	SB	BA	SA
1936	StLA	152	576	145	174	40	11	20	73	12	.302	.514
1937		155	571	103	175	36	7	29	118	8	.306	.546
1938		149	534	119	155	25	7	34	118	10	.290	.554
1939		151	526	90	142	25	2	15	84	4	.270	.411
1940		150	523	92	143	29	5	20	87	9	.273	.463
1941		154*	584	108	149	33	9	17	84	6	.255	.430
1942		143	541	108	148	39	4	7	55	6	.274	.399
1943	StLA	105	379	43	88	11	3	3	25	5	.232	.301
	WasA	8	30	4	9	0	0	0	4	0	.300	.300
	Year	113	409	47	97	11	3	3	29	5	.237	.301
1944	WasA	12	44	4	7	3	0	0	3	0	.159	.227
1945		119	375	49	79	12	0	8	53	2	.211	.307
12 years		1582	5730	1070	1558	309	62	178	829	69	.272	.441

*Led league

All-Star Game

1937　　American　　　　　　Selected, did not play

ELBIE FLETCHER

Elbie Fletcher (Pittsburgh Pirates Photo Library).

Gold Glove
NL All-Star 1943

"*My first year in the big leagues I got $3,700 and I couldn't believe you could make that much money having fun.*"
— Elbie Fletcher

Buck Jordan was a good first baseman. He was the regular at that position for the Boston Braves from 1933 through 1936, during which time he batted an even .300.

The 1936 season had been his best yet. He reached personal highs in several offensive categories: hits, runs, walks, and BA (.323) and he fanned only 22 times in 555 at bats.

And he could field. In '36 he was second in fielding average, assists, and total chances per game and led the National League in double plays.

Unfortunately for Buck (his given names were Baxter Byerly, so a nickname was a necessity), however, the Braves had a 20-year-old first baseman playing at Buffalo in the International League who had many things going for him: He had a three-year minor league average of .335 (.344 in 1936), he was brilliant in the field, and he was a local Boston (Dorchester) boy. He was Elbie Fletcher.

Elbie's play made Jordan expendable and three weeks into the '37 season Buck was sold to Cincinnati. Fletcher was only 21, but he played first base as few of any age ever had.

(The year of 1937 was a good year for Braves' rookies. In additional to Fletcher, Vince DiMaggio took over in center field and two of the four 20-game winners in the National League anchored the pitching staff, the unlikely first year duo of 33-year-old Jim Turner [20-11, league-leading 2.38] and 30-year-old Lou Fette [20-10, 2.88].)

Elbie's offensive production that first season fell a little short of what Jordan had done in '36, but his defense was the best the NL had seen at least since Bill Terry's heyday. He led in putouts, double plays, and total chances per game and was second in assists and average.

His defense stayed and his offense improved in '38, but in '39 the Braves acquired the veteran Buddy Hassett and he took over at first. Hassett wouldn't strike out and he hit for a higher average than Fletcher, but even so Elbie was a far more potent offensive force (more power, more walks, more run production) and a vastly better glove man.

Two first basemen weren't needed, so Elbie was sent to the Pirates, where he had four solid seasons, including an All-Star Game start, before World War II interfered. Like so many others, he lost two prime years to Uncle Sam.

It was with Pittsburgh that Fletcher developed into one of the better offensive forces in the NL. He drove in 104 runs in 1940, scored over 90 runs three times, led the league in walks twice (averaging over 100 a year while a Pirate regular), and led the league in on-base average three times in a row (averaging over .400 as a Pirate).

The acquisition of Hank Greenberg in 1947 ended Elbie's days as an everyday Pirate. (It was a singularly unsuccessful move as Pittsburgh fell into the cellar for the first time in 30 years.) After the season Elbie was sold to the

Indians but an injury prevented him from playing there and he made a curtain call back with the Braves in '49.

Illness caused him to leave baseball in 1950 but he looks back on his career warmly and proudly.

I heard a story years ago that you initiated a write-in campaign in a newspaper to draw the Braves' attention to you.

Elbie Fletcher: (Laughs) What had happened, the Boston newspaper, the *Record-American*, ran a contest for people to write in recommending certain sandlot or high school players that they had seen and tell why possibly they might have the qualifications to eventually become a big league ballplayer.

I didn't come from a big family but I had a lot of relatives around and I just made sure that they all sent in a coupon recommending me. I don't know how much impact that had, but nevertheless I won the contest, which was a free trip to spring training with the Boston Braves. That was in 1934.

I was president of my class in high school and they let me off to go to spring training and down there they had an open-air school — Miss Aikens' Open-Air School, I'll never forget it. Some mornings I'd go with Bill McKechnie's daughter or Babe Ruth's daughter and we'd go off to school early in the morning and then at 10:00 I'd be free and that's when practice would start.

You must have impressed them. They signed you.

(Laughs) It turned out that way because I went back and finished my high school and I graduated on a Friday night, I got a bus Saturday morning and went to Harrisburg (New York–Penn. League) and opened up there Saturday night.

And ended up in Boston at the end of the year.

Yeah, I came back at the end of the year. Our season ended and they just had me come back to finish out the season.

That must have been pretty exciting for an 18-year-old.

It sure was. Of course, baseball is the one thing I always wanted to do but you never know whether you have the ability or not, but fortunately my ability did develop and it worked out just fine.

Your first full year with Boston was 1937 but in '39 they got Buddy Hassett and you were nearly given to Pittsburgh.

I was sold. In fact, (William E.) Benswanger (Pirates president) called me up in the office the next morning after I was sold and showed me a check for $20,000 that he had to pay for me. I looked at a check for $20,000 and I couldn't believe it. In those days, that was an awful lot of money plus there was another ballplayer that was involved (minor league shortstop Bill Schuster went to Boston).

In 1938 with the Braves, you, Tony Cuccinello, and Max West hit three consecutive home runs. None of the three of you were known for your power.

Max West had pretty good power. Tony was something like me — he might hit 15 home runs or something like that. But New York — the Polo Grounds was a different kind of ballpark. If you hit the lines there you're gonna be getting home runs.

On June 6, 1941, you equalled the modern National League record with 21 putouts in a nine-inning game. (Ernie Banks broke it on May 9, 1963, with 22.)

I think Rip Sewell pitched that ballgame.

Do you recall anything else about that game?

When you're setting records, you're not really aware of it — you don't even think about it. Then after it's happened you can go back and say, "Geez, they were really popping that ball on the ground all the way around." I don't think there were over three fly outs in the whole game.

There is little doubt that you were the top fielding first baseman of your day, but here's a tough question: Were you the best fielding first baseman ever?

Put it this way: I felt, down deep, that there was nobody that could hit a ball by me or throw one by me. Of course, they did, but this was the attitude I had. I used to tell my infielders, "Throw the ball bad to make me look good."

I just had that feeling inside of me that I was the top first baseman. Naturally I made some errors but that's how I felt.

There was a lot of ones that might have had a better (fielding) average, but they never could move. Like Johnny Mize, for instance; he might have a higher average, but if you hit a ball two feet on either side of him he didn't move. You can't make errors unless you make good tries.

Fielding average alone is a poor measure of fielding ability.

That's true.

Just going by stories I've heard and things that I've read and looking at your record, in your time there was no one better. And from examining the records, if the Gold Glove Award was given in your day, you probably would have won five of them (1937, '41, '42, '43, '46, and maybe '38).

Yes. I think I would have been entitled to them.

You know, there were some pretty good first basemen around in my day. (Dolf) Camilli was a good first baseman; I always enjoyed playing against him and watching him. Frank McCormick was a good first baseman.

Hassett wasn't bad.

I have no comment on Buddy. When (Casey) Stengel made that decision to take Hassett over me, with the record that I compiled against what Hassett had, I think there was a little bit of a buddy relationship there. Of course, it was all to my advantage. The greatest thing that ever happened to me was being traded from Boston to Pittsburgh.

In 1940 you had your biggest offensive season. Your 104 RBI's were fourth in the league.

Ebie Fletcher (center) being congratulated after hitting home run (Pittsburgh Pirates Photo Library).

With only 139 base hits.
Where did you bat in the lineup?
We varied around. I'd go like three, four, and five. It would depend on who was there — like when (Ralph) Kiner was there he was the big gun.

Usually, the Waners would go one-two and Arky Vaughan would be right in there as a good third man and I'd be fourth or fifth most of my career.

You were voted the starting first baseman in the 1943 All-Star game. That must have been pretty exciting.

It was that. They started me and you know who I had to face? It was Dutch Leonard and of course all he was firing up there was knuckle balls.

(Babe) Dahlgren came in after me. He was a local Philadelphia first baseman at that time.

That's a horrible pitch (the knuckle ball) to try to hit at. You ought to try. This Charlie Hough they've got now — he's just amazing. They've been able to show you on TV. They slow it down to actually show what that does, the revolutions of the ball. It's an amazing thing to see. You just can't take that real vicious swing, you gotta kind of dance around with the ball and try to make contact.

After 1943 you went in the Navy for two years and played at Bainbridge, Maryland, with a lot of awfully good ballplayers and you were the leading hitter. Buddy Blattner, Eddie Miksis, and Dick Bartell were there. Who else?

Bob Scheffing was catching — good ballplayer. We had a couple of top minor league players and we had a couple of good pitchers: (Bobby) Coombs from New York (Giants), Maxie Wilson, a *very* crafty left-handed pitcher. Dick Sisler was there. We had a good ballclub.

You came out and returned to Pittsburgh and they traded you to Cleveland for the 1948 season.

Yes, the year that they were World's Champions.

What happened there?

They had Eddie Robinson over there but the trade was just fine with me because they had some confidence that I was gonna be their first baseman. Everything was going great in spring training and I hit a ball to right-center and I was rounding second base and instead of looking at the third base coach I was watching the ball and the way I hit the bag I broke my metatarsal arch.

In those days, the trainers never took care of their ballplayers. You know what they did? They tried to build up my arch by crossing bandaids so when I put my shoe on this was supposed to force the arch up. Of course, I couldn't even move and they did nothing. They never did in those days.

As a result, when it came cut-down time I was the guy that was gonna go. I was going into New York — I was gonna go to to Ebbets Field and try to see if I couldn't get a job and I was hurting. I was walking down the street and I saw this little store that said, "Arch Supports — this will cure you overnight" and stuff like that. I went in there and bought one of those things and I put it on and I went out and I worked out in Brooklyn. I thought I looked pretty good but they didn't have a place for me.

Before I left, I got a call from Carl Hubbell to go out to Minneapolis, so with a bonus and a salary it didn't look bad at all.

Then the following year I started out in Jersey City because I wanted to get closer to home, and the whole family came down to Jersey City. We just got the food in and the kids to bed and the phone rang and it was Boston telling me to report the next day to Chicago.

My wife had to repack everything, put the kids back in the car, drive all the way back to Boston. I got a plane and I'm in Chicago the next day ready to play. That was quite an experience.

Did you call it quits after that year?

No. I had a pretty good year with Boston and I was pretty disappointed they didn't give me a shot (in 1950), but that's the way baseball is.

I got contacted by Los Angeles out in the Pacific Coast League and with their bonus and salary it was more money than I made playing in Boston. I was out there and I was hitting about .360 or .380 and one of the boys contracted the mumps. I thought that I'd had the mumps back when I was a kid. Now I'm about 34 years old and all of a sudden I came up with the mumps. We were coming home from Seattle and I was shaking all over. I saw the doctor the next day and he said, "You've got the mumps."

I was so weak I couldn't play. I played a little bit but I was so tired I couldn't swing a bat.

So at the end of the season, they (the Angels) were no longer interested and I had kind of lost my desire. My legs were beginning to hurt and when your legs hurt you're hurting all over. I said to my wife, "Let's pack up the kids and get back to Boston. I'll got get a job and we'll start all over." And that's exactly what I did.

What did you go into?

Many different things. I sold industrial lubricants and I had no idea what that was. (Laughs) I sold furniture at Payne's Furniture Company here, which was a big furniture store.

Then, all of a sudden, I got a break and I got a job as Recreation Director for the city of Melrose. I was looking for a job that had a retirement fund to go along with my baseball pension, which I was fortunate enough to get involved in, so I was 25 years as Recreation Director and I retired from the city of Melrose about ten years ago.

With the baseball pension and the city pension and two Social Securities, I'm living pretty good.

The funny thing, the (baseball) pension that I'm getting is more than *twice* what I made playing! There'll never be a poor ballplayer again.

I never made any money, as far as what they're talking today, but to me it was fun. My first year in the big leagues I got $3,700 and I couldn't *believe* you could make that much money having fun. (Laughs) Money was never an object. We knew Babe Ruth made dough. We didn't worry about it. It was fun all the time. It's big business today. I think the players are different, also.

Is there one game that stands out?

Like I tell everybody, to me anytime I got a base hit to win a ballgame or made an outstanding play that was instrumental in winning a ballgame, that to me was a distinct thrill.

But I can recall playing Chicago; I think we beat them maybe 3-to-1 or 3-to-2. The first two times I had hit home runs off a jinx of mine, Claude Passeau, a righthander. I used to have a hell of a time trying to hit him; all of a sudden it turned around. I used to call him "Cousin."

The third one I hit off the top of the wall in right-center for a double, so I drove in all the runs.

Was Passeau the toughest on you?

He was one of the toughest, but all of a sudden after a couple of years it turned around. He used to say, "If I faced nine guys like you, I'd win 30 ballgames."

The thing of it is, when you're going well, you don't really single out one that gives you a lot of trouble, but when you're in a slump the ball looks like an aspirin. When you're going good it looks like a softball. When you're in a slump. I don't care what you do, you can't get out of it.

Who was the best player you saw?

I thought the best looking player I played with was Paul Waner. He was just a magician. I remember one day I think he got six hits. We used to say, "Gee, he's got a special bat." He had us pick out the bat before he went to the plate. "What do you want me to use?" We'd pick out one and it didn't make any difference.

The best all-around player I played against was (Stan) Musial. I thought he was great. He could do a little of everything; he had the speed, he was a great hitter, he was a great competitor.

There were an awful lot of great ballplayers in that era. There were so many great players there could have been *30* players that I thought were really outstanding. Enos Slaughter was great, Terry Moore was great, (Pete) Reiser, Duke Snider — fellows like that. You start to write out a list and all of a sudden you find, "Gee, I've got 50 players that look great." I probably could name more good players than I could bad players.

Of course, everything's different today. The gloves are different, the ball is different, the bats are different, the playing fields are different, the conditioning of athletes is different. They used to tell us, "When you go home this winter, don't do anything to maybe get yourself muscle-bound." Now that's the way they do — everyone's pumping iron.

Today I see these guys swinging from their ass after two strikes with men in scoring position when all you need is a fly ball, a ground ball, or something. The home runs are what pays off.

When I see guys now hitting .210, .220 that couldn't even have got into the ballpark, but today, with expansion and whatnot, if a guy has a little power he plays. Also, pitchers that don't even have .500 records are making this kind of dough; it's amazing.

I think back, I wonder about the pitchers in my day that were 18-and-10 or 18-and-12; they were probably getting $7,500, something like that. What must they be thinking today?

Another thing, in those days, I can remember having a good year over in Pittsburgh and I think I was making seven (thousand), so Benswanger, at the end of the season, said, "I'll tell you what I'll do. You sign right now, I'll give you $10,000. If you don't, when you get your contract it'll only be for nine." What the hell could you do? They used to tell you what you're gonna make and if you don't like it, stay home.

The owners dominated the players and now it's just the opposite. I'm wondering when a medium can be reached. These guys are getting seven million or six million or five million a year — unbelievable!

Of course, if it hadn't been for television this could never happen, but TV has lost a few bucks on some of the World Series coverage and their packages in the future may not be so good. There may come that day of reckoning. I think that's why management's trying to get away from these long-term contracts because how do we know five years down the road whether that income's gonna be there?

Who was the best manager you played for?

To me the greatest manager was Bill McKechnie. I thought he was the finest manager I ever played for and I think the finest manager *anybody* played for. Not just his record, but the character of the guy. When I went down there in 1934, just a bush-leaguer along with a lot of others, he treated us just like we were his own kids. That's the interest he took. He watched over us all the time. You know, that was the first time we'd been out of town and had a couple of bucks; he wanted to be sure that we didn't get with the wrong crowd or this and that. A guy like that, you don't find too many of them. Today a manager's not that interested.

Do you receive much fan mail?

I do pretty well, considering I've been out of it so long. I probably get, oh, eight or ten a week — requests for autographs, those that have baseball cards or they'll enclose a picture they might have. I'm kind of flattered in a way that, after the honeymoon is over, they still remember.

Any regrets?

No. I couldn't possibly have any regrets because I enjoyed the game so much. I loved every minute of it. I looked forward every day to going out there. What could anybody regret? You just disregard the things that go wrong. There were managers that I wasn't wild about and they probably weren't wild about me, but heavens, that's part of the game.

* * *

We can't answer the question of whether Elbie Fletcher is the best fielding first baseman ever. Changes in gloves and fields over the years make across-the-eras comparisons very difficult, if not impossible. We can, however, show that he was certainly the best of his day.

The accompanying lists all the regular first basemen who were contemporaries of Elbie before the war. We've only considered the seasons in which both they and Elbie were regulars at the same time. They are arranged by TC/G.

The fact that there are only fractional differences between these numbers is misleading. The major league schedule was 154 games when these guys were playing, so a difference of 0.5 TC/G equals 77 chances over the course of a season. Therefore, Elbie made from 65 (McCormick) to 156 (McQuinn) *more* plays a season than these other guys. That would save a lot of runs.

He just may have been the best ever.

FIELDING COMPARISONS:
ELBIE FLETCHER VS. CONTEMPORARY MAJOR LEAGUE FIRST BASEMEN

	G Avg.	G Led	PO Avg.	PO Led	A Avg.	A Led	E Avg.	E Led	DP Avg.	DP Led	TC/G Avg.	TC/G Led	FA	Led
Elbie Fletcher (1937–43)	146.0	2	1461.7	3	111.6	6	11.9	1	120.3	1	10.86	5	.9925	1
Frank McCormick (1938–43)	146.7	3	1428.2	4	95.2	0	7.7	0	134.0	4	10.44	0	.9950	3
Joe Kuhel (1937–43)	136.3	1	1289.0	0	84.4	0	11.6	0	116.1	1	10.17	0	.9917	0
Dolf Camilli (1937–42)	145.2	2	1356.5	0	97.5	1	12.0	0	114.3	0	10.10	0	.9918	1
Johnny Mize (1937–42)	141.5	0	1313.2	0	81.0	0	13.5	2	108.5	0	9.95	0	.9904	1
George McQuinn (1938–43)	140.5	1	1269.0	1	105.0	2	10.3	0	121.0	1	9.85	0	.9925	2

ELBURT PRESTON FLETCHER
Born March 18, 1916, Milton, MA
Died March 9, 1994, Milton, MA
Ht. 6'   Wt. 180   Batted and Threw Left

Year	Team	G	AB	R	H	2B	3B	HR	RBI	SB	BA	SA
1934	BosN	8	4	4	2	0	0	0	0	1	.500	.500
1935		39	148	12	35	7	1	1	9	1	.236	.318
1937		148	539	56	133	22	4	1	38	3	.247	.308
1938		147	529	71	144	24	7	6	48	5	.272	.378
1939	BosN	35	106	14	26	2	0	0	6	1	.245	.264
	PitN	102	370	49	112	23	4	12	71	3	.303	.484
1940	PitN	147	510	94	139	22	7	16	104	5	.273	.437
1941		151	521	95	150	29	13	11	74	5	.288	.457
1942		145	506	86	146	22	5	7	57	0	.289	.393
1943		154*	544	91	154	24	5	9	70	1	.283	.395
1946		148	532	72	136	25	8	4	66	4	.256	.355
1947		69	157	22	38	9	1	1	22	2	.242	.331
1949		122	413	57	108	19	3	11	51	1	.262	.402
12 years		1415	4879	723	1323	228	58	79	616	32	.271	.390

*Led league

All-Star Game

Year	Team	G	AB	R	H	2B	3B	HR	RBI	SB	BA	SA
1943	National	1	2	0	0	0	0	0	0	0	.000	.000

MEL HARDER

Mel Harder (second from left) with the Indians' 1961 brain trust: (l. to r.) coach Mel McGaha, manager Jimmy Dykes, coach Luke Appling (courtesy of Cleveland Indians).

Art Teacher
AL All-Star 1934, 1935, 1936, 1937

> *"I liked to teach. I liked to sit down with a pitcher and talk to him about pitching, about the art of pitching."*
> — Mel Harder

The list of players who spent 20 years or more in the major leagues is short. Fewer than 100 men out of the 13,000 or so who have played major league ball ever lasted that long. Another handful spent 20 years in uniform as major league managers or coaches, but very few played for 20 years and then also spent another 20 years on the field in a non-playing capacity.

The membership of this latter group totals one: Mel Harder.

Guys like Jimmy Dykes, Charlie Grimm, and Cap Anson each had 20 years as both players and leaders, but there was considerable overlap as playing managers. Harder is the only one to have separate 20-year careers in each capacity.

Mel spent 20 years with the Indians as one of the top hurlers in the American League. He went largely unnoticed, however, because the Indians played fairly unremarkable ball for the whole two decades. For 17 of those seasons the Tribe was either third, fourth, or fifth and averaged 20½ games back. The other three years they were second, sixth, and seventh.

From 1932 through 1939, Mel won between 15 and 22 games each year. He was the *only* major league pitcher to win at least 15 for those eight years.

Also, he was the *only* American League hurler and the *only* major league right-hander to win in double figures in each year of the decade of the '30s. (Two NL southpaws, Carl Hubbell and Larry French, joined him in this distinction.) Remember, this was a decade that saw such pitchers as Lefty Grove, Lefty Gomez, Red Ruffing, Ted Lyons, Dizzy Dean, Wes Ferrell, Tommy Bridges, Lon Warneke, and Van Mungo reach their peaks.

Harder won 223 games and lost 186 in his 20 years, but in the 15 in which he took his regular turn on the mound he won 208 and lost 169. Either way, compare his record to that of many of those in the Hall of Fame. Just for kicks, here's the won-lost records of a few Hall of Famers from the live-ball era compared with Mel's:

Pitcher	Yrs	W	L	Pitcher	Yrs	W	L
Ted Lyons	21	260	230	Don Drysdale	14	209	166
Whitey Ford	16	236	106	Dazzy Vance	16	197	140
MEL HARDER	20	223	186	Lefty Gomez	14	189	102
Jesse Haines	19	210	158	Dizzy Dean	12	150	83

As good as he was against the rest of the American League, he really showed his stuff when he faced the rival National League. Look at his All-Star Game record at the end of the chapter. The greatest pitchers in baseball have pitched in these games and *no* one in the history of All-Star competition has a record to compare. Look it up.

In 1934, his first All-Star Game, he turned in possibly the best performance the game has ever seen. He faced some pretty fair country hitters: Mel

Ott, Paul Waner, Chuck Klein, Bill Terry, Billy Herman, Arkie Vaughan, Frank Frisch, Pie Traynor, and Al Lopez, *all* of them Hall of Fame members. In five innings, obviously, he saw some of these guys twice and the only one to get a hit was Herman. (Probably not coincidentally, Billy had one of the best batting records in All-Star play. You can look that up, too.)

But 1934 was the year Carl Hubbell chose to strike out five of history's greatest hitters in a row and it was this performance that made the headlines, captured the imaginations of the fans, and is remembered today. Harder's job went unnoticed during the game and in the reports that followed it, but the next day syndicated New York sports columnist Paul Gallico, who had heaped great praise on Hubbell the previous day, looked over an account of the game and wrote:

> This department owes some kind of apology to a party by the name of Mel Harder, who throws curve balls righthanded for the Cleveland Indians, an American League team.
>
> Somehow his work in the all-star game didn't look as showy or exciting as Hubbell's performance, but it must have been. It looks much better on paper.
>
> … There is a considerable pitching record.

And even with an annual look at his offerings, the National League sluggers never solved the riddle of his pitches sufficiently to score a run. It remains "a considerable pitching record."

Once Mel stepped off the mound for good he immediately began his 23-year coaching career. The list of pitchers he worked with or helped develop reads like a Hurling Who's Who: Bob Lemon, Bob Feller, Early Wynn, Mike Garcia, Herb Score, Gene Bearden, Dick Donovan, Mudcat Grant, Jim Perry, Jim Maloney, Gary Nolan, Dick Drago, Hal Newhouser, Don Mossi, etc., etc.

Just on numbers, you compare favorably to many in the Hall of Fame. Do you think you deserve Hall of Fame consideration?

Mel Harder: You never know how your record stands up to others. Some are in with less victories. But Dizzy Dean, for instance, he was a great pitcher and he probably would have gone on to win a lot more ballgames if he hadn't been injured in that All-Star Game. And then he came back too soon and injured his arm.

You won 20 games twice and were remarkably consistent for 15 years, except for a couple of injuries. You won more games than relative contemporaries such as Haines, Vance, and Gomez.

Yes. I started pitching regularly in '30 and along about '32 I started to pitch pretty good. I started reaching my peak along about '33-'34-'35. In '36

I had 12 victories and three defeats at All-Star time and I kind of figured I had a chance to win between 20 and 25 ballgames because I still had July, August, and September. I was pitching good ball but then I hurt my shoulder in the first game after the All-Star Game and my arm was never the same after that.

You were still a front-line pitcher for another decade.

Well, yes. But that's when my troubles started and I think I could have added another 10, 12, or more wins in '36.

Then I came back in '37 and I had a pretty good year; I think I won 15. Along in '39 my elbow started bothering me. It bothered me quite a bit there in '39 and '40. We had a chance to win the pennant in '40. I think if I could have had a normal year with a good arm we could have won it.

I had my arm operated on in the fall of '41. Then I pitched another six years. I struggled quite a bit then. But my arm was really never the same after '36.

Your All-Star record is the best of any pitcher in history. This is generally overlooked, yet you were never scored on in four games.

'34, '5, '6, and '7. I pitched 13 innings and didn't allow any runs.

There were some pretty good hitters in the National League in those days.

There weren't any .300 hitters; they were all *.350* hitters. They had Traynor, Bill Terry, Mel Ott, Chuck Klein, Paul Waner.

The game in '34 was the one in which Hubbell did his great job. I pitched five innings and allowed one hit and no runs, but everybody was so interested in Hubbell's feat that they never paid any attention to mine.

You were the winning pitcher in that game.

Yes. Hubbell pitched the first three innings for the National League and they got a few hits off of him but he had that one streak where he struck out all those great hitters and that's what made the ballgame.

The New York writers, I don't think they even knew I was in the game.

You played your whole career on a team that was only mediocre.

We always had good clubs but we lacked the one or two players who could really make our club a pennant winner. We usually stayed in the race until July or so and then we started to taper off.

You had some big stars there. What was missing?

Our trouble was sometimes our defense wasn't too hot. And, also, some of those years the Yankees were so good if we won, in a 154-game schedule, 88 or 90 games we might be 10 or more games behind. It made everyone look bad—the whole league. They maybe won the pennant by 10, 12, 15 games.

And starting in '29 the Philadelphia Athletics had that great club for four years. And then along came Detroit. We were always battling someone like that. We finished third and fourth all the time.

We had some good hitters and some good pitchers, but defensively that hurt us a lot. An extra couple of steps in the outfield means so much and it's the same way on the infield. You can have a .990 fielding average and be a

Mel Harder (courtesy of *The National Pastime*).

weak link on the club. I remember some fellows who could hit but they couldn't move off a dime, you know. Nobody paid much attention to those things except your own ballclub, of course. The fans didn't pay too much attention, all they cared about was the guy who could hit .300.

You were a regular member of the pitching staff at 20 and had been up for two years then, so you didn't spend a great deal of time in the minors. What kind of minor league record did you have?

I started in 1927 with Omaha. I first signed with Omaha and I went to spring training with the club and I stayed with them after the season started for about two weeks or so and they decided to send me over to Dubuque, Iowa. That was a Class D league. I was over there around May 1st.

In those years the Mississippi Valley League was a non-option league; they had to own all their ballplayers. No club had any affiliation. They could get players from other clubs but they had to buy them.

I was sent there by Omaha, but with strings attached. In fact, I was owned by Omaha and I wasn't supposed to be on that club (Dubuque) then.

I had a good start there. I won 13 games in two months and the club was in first place. Well, somebody found out I was still owned by Omaha and they had a big meeting and threw out my 13 wins and that put Dubuque back in third or fourth place. They still went on to win the pennant. They had a good club.

But I went back to Omaha. I finished the season there — I think I won about four games and lost about six or seven. In August, the Cleveland Indians bought me. The White Sox were after me and the Cardinals, also, but Cleveland made the best offer.

I reported to the Indians in spring training in 1928. I stayed with them that year when I was 18. I had a pretty good spring training. Nobody paid much attention to me, but when our exhibition schedule started I went out and shut a few clubs out in my three innings a few times. And I threw a lot of ground balls — my fastball was a natural sinker. Hitters always topped the ball and I had good luck with it. I didn't have much of a curveball in those years.

I kept pitching pretty good in spring training and finally Roger Peckinpaugh decided to keep me on the club. I was just used in relief because I was young. I pitched in 23 games in 1928.

A couple of hitters I got to pitch against were Ty Cobb and Tris Speaker when they were finishing up with the Philadelphia Athletics. I really remember that!

In 1929 on August 1st, New Orleans, our farm club, needed a pitcher. They were in a pennant race. The Indians decided to send me down to help them out, so I went down and I was down there six weeks and I won seven games and lost two games. We lost out to Birmingham by a game for the pennant. I rejoined the Indians on September 15, a couple of weeks before the season was over.

In all my years with the Indians, that was the only six weeks I was farmed out.

In your time, who was the toughest batter for you and who was the best batter you ever saw?

The toughest hitters that I had to face were Lou Gehrig and Charlie Gehringer and Bill Dickey, all left-hand hitters. And all *good* hitters. They were the type of hitters that would hit to all fields instead of just trying to pull the ball all the time. That's what made it tougher for me because throwing my fastball sinker I pitched away a lot to left-handers — on the outside part of the plate. Of course, when a left-hander tried to pull me it was mostly a ground ball, but those three guys would take me to left field a lot, even Gehrig, especially with two strikes on him. Those three guys gave me most of the trouble I had.

As far as the best hitter I saw, I think I'd have to choose Gehrig, although I pitched against Babe Ruth a lot. He was a fellow who was going for home runs all the time. Gehrig was a power hitter himself, but he was a different type of hitter. He was tough.

Who was the best pitcher you saw?

I'd say Walter Johnson, but I missed by one year seeing him pitch. I played for Walter a couple of years in Cleveland and I saw him pitch batting practice a lot of times and he could still throw pretty good then. I got to thinking if he was throwing like that at his age after being out for a few years, why those stories about him throwing that ball so hard must have all been true. In my opinion, Walter Johnson was the greatest.

In our league, though, I think Ted Lyons was one of the tops and I think if Bob Feller had those four years back that he spent in the service he would have won 350 games. That was right in his prime. He was pitching great and 20 to 25 (wins) was nothing for him.

You became a coach in 1947.

I pitched up till, I think, the latter part of June. I had won six games and lost four — I wasn't doing too badly. I still had three months to go. I think I could have won another six games or something like that. Twelve wins isn't bad. Look at what they give now for 12 games.

But we were in fourth place and going nowhere and Bill Veeck and Lou Boudreau wanted to make a few changes and start some young pitchers. Two of those guys were out in the bullpen — one was Bob Lemon and the other was Steve Gromek. All Lemon did was win nine out of 11 starts, I think.

I could understand that because I was pretty close to the end of my career. Veeck said that after the season he was going to make me pitching coach of the entire system, the Indians and minor leagues, too. So I started to do that in 1948.

I went to spring training and worked with the Indians' pitchers for about three weeks or so, then I went to where the minor league clubs were training and stayed there for a few weeks. Then I came back to Cleveland and after a week or so I went to Oklahoma City and worked with the pitchers for a while. Then I got a call to come back to the Indians. They put me coaching first base and I stayed with the Indians the rest of the season.

They had Bill McKechnie and Muddy Ruel on the club then and Muddy Ruel was working with the pitchers quite a bit.

When did you become the full-time pitching coach?

1949.

The 1954 Indians—that's been called the best pitching staff ever. Do you think so?

Yes, I do. I think overall that that was the best, with our starters and our middle men and our two relievers, Narleski and Mossi.

You really had about an eight-man staff, so you probably got the maximum out of those eight. You had Lemon, Wynn, and Garcia, of course, but you had some "if's." Feller was on the way out.

He was getting to the end of his career and he had problems now and then.

How did you determine how to use him? He couldn't be an every fourth or fifth day starter at that point.

We used Lemon and Garcia and Wynn often with three days' rest. And we had Art Houtteman in there, too.

Feller was used as the schedule indicated. Al Lopez would use him like that. We figured he needed extra rest. (Feller pitched in 19 games, all starts, and went 13-3.)

The other guys even pitched on two days' rest a couple of times late in the season. And when we had off days, we'd just use the three of them.

You had Art Houtteman and Hal Newhouser, both Detroit cast-offs. You took both of them and got maximum performance.

Houtteman was in good shape with our club. His arm felt good and we spot started him and he had plenty of rest. Also, we used him as the long man in the bullpen. He pitched good ball for us. He could give the other starters an extra day.

Newhouser we used in the latter parts of ballgames to start an inning. And he had plenty of rest, too.

You had two rookies, Mossi and Narleski. Mossi had been a successful minor league starter and was later a successful Major League starter. Was it difficult for him to adjust to the bullpen?

When we went to spring training in '54 Narleski threw fast and had a good arm, but he didn't come in with any big record. Lopez kind of liked him, he had a sneaky fastball and good control.

Mossi, every time we worked out always complained of his arm. We couldn't use him for the first part of spring training. He wore copper bracelets, that sort of stuff, supposed to be good for arthritis.

Finally, Mossi and I got together and we decided he couldn't throw too many innings, but he needed to strengthen the arm. So I had him throw for ten straight days, not too much, and he said he never felt so good.

He had a sneaky fastball and that's what caught Lopez's eye. Both of them did a real good job.

Neither of these two pitched the number of games that relievers pitch today.

We could go into the seventh inning and if our starter looked like he was losing it we'd get both of them up and bring in the one we needed — Narleski if a right-hander was up and Mossi if a left-hander was up.

We had a lot of complete ballgames (77), so that made a lot of difference in your bullpen. The way they do it now you can be shutting somebody out in the sixth or seventh inning, two to nothing or something like that, and they'll make a change. That's silly.

I remember when they started counting pitches. Someone on our club turned to me and asked, "How many pitches has he thrown?" I said, "Hell, I don't know." I always went by how they looked and if they were getting wild or beginning to lose their stuff.

Back in the early '30s when I first started pitching we'd just go until we got tired. Sometimes you'd get by the sixth inning and you could hardly walk out to the mound, but then all of a sudden you'd get your second wind and you'd pitch the last three innings in good shape.

I pitched Opening Day one year down in St. Louis—14 innings. They wouldn't let you do that today. I beat the Browns, 2-to-1.

What do you think of artificial turf?

That's changed baseball quite a bit. Ground balls go through, you very seldom get a bad hop. On natural turf you can get those bad hops. And the grass can be mowed differently to speed up or slow down ground balls and be watered differently to do the same thing. And it would be different between ballparks. Foul lines could be fixed, slope them in or out. You can't do any of that with the artificial turf.

What about the designated hitter?

I'm against that. I think the National League has the best system, it keeps baseball just like it's supposed to be. You have pretty good hitting pitchers. Around the seventh inning in a well-pitched game if you get a couple of runners on and the pitcher comes up, then the manager's got to get off of his fanny and make a decision.

Al Lopez was a very successful manager. How do you compare him to Casey Stengel?

I think Lopez ranks right up there with the best. He had the knack of evaluating talent. He'd see something in a ballplayer that maybe another man couldn't. He had his way of reading ballplayers — whether they were phonies or not, or whether they'd put out for you. He was great in handling pitching staffs. He just knew a lot about baseball and he knew how to handle players. He wouldn't push them, but if something happened he'd pull them in his office right away and he'd tell them right quick.

He had a lot of respect from the players.

Casey did, too, but Casey had some good clubs. But, still, he made moves that a lot of other managers wouldn't have. I coached for him one year with the Mets.

With the Yankees, he had a knack of remembering if a hitter could hit certain pitchers or if they played good against certain clubs, and if they did, he'd have them in the lineup. He had all that in his head.

Did you ever have a desire to be a manager?

No. I wasn't even too crazy about some of the jobs the coaches had to do.

I liked to teach. I liked to sit down with a pitcher and talk to him about pitching, about the art of pitching. That's what I liked to do. I liked to get a pitcher on the sidelines and watch him throw and we'd talk about how to hold certain pitches, how to keep you elbow away from your body, and different little things that help a pitcher when he was out there on the mound. That's what I liked.

Let's talk about some of the pitchers you helped over the years — Bob Lemon.
I worked quite a bit with Bob. We worked on his curveball.

Bob had a terrific sinker. When he was playing third base he'd throw the ball to first base and it would sink. Same thing when he played center field. When he was in the Navy, he pitched a few games out there in Hawaii and I think it was Bill Dickey who suggested we look at him as a pitcher. That's when I started working with Bob.

Bob had a few faults. He thought he had to throw hard when he was pitching and the harder he threw the less his ball would sink. So we had to find his natural delivery so when he did throw a fastball it would sink all the time.

We worked on his curveball, the spin of it, and he had a terrific curve and he came up with a great slider. His slider was something a lot of pitchers wish they had for their curveball.

Mike Garcia in 1949 had a great rookie season. What did you do for him?
We worked on his control and his curveball. He had to come up with a change of pace. With his natural ability, he came along pretty fast. His control improved. He was a good man to teach, he picked up things fast. He had a terrific fastball and a good delivery, threw everything right at the hitter — that kind of intimidated them a little.

We tried to correct him from falling off to the left of the mound on his pitches. That kind of messed him up a little for a while, so we went back to letting him throw natural. We never talked to him about that again. He was a little weak on balls hit back through the mound because he'd fall over to the left side, but he had to do that to get the good stuff on the ball.

You had another pitcher in '49 who had been around for years with a bad team — Early Wynn. He had had only limited success, but he became a dominating pitcher after he joined the Indians.

When Early joined the Indians from Washington, he was a good pitcher. He had a couple of good years over there.

He was a fastball pitcher and he had a little curveball but he threw a knuckleball in there, too. But he didn't change up much on his pitches. When he got over to Cleveland, I talked to him about it. He was the type of guy who was anxious to learn something about the art of pitching, so we worked on a curveball, to get a little more spin on it, worked on a slider, and we kind of forgot about his knuckleball for a while. He only used the knuckleball to show the hitter he had it, as sort of a change.

But then he got to throw his fastball with two different speeds, he threw his slider with different speeds, and he threw his curveball with different speeds. That's the art of pitching. He'd make pitches that you'd swear that hitters could take pretty good swings at, but the changing of speeds is what really helped him a lot, made him such a really great pitcher. And he developed good control of all his pitches.

He would never give in to a hitter, no matter the count. He just had so much confidence in his control that it didn't make any difference to him.

You had a pitcher a few years later, kind of an old rookie who really only gave you one good year: Dave Hoskins.

Everything went good for him in the good year he had. Like Gene Bearden in '48, everything he threw was just in the right spot, then in '49 that same pitch was a ball and when he'd come up in the strike zone they'd tee off on him. The harder he tried to get his old form back, the worse he got. Every time he threw that knuckleball he had, it was either a ball or up in the strike zone too high. We tried to straighten him out a lot of times, but he just didn't seem to come around.

It was the same way with Dave. Everything went right for him in '53 and nothing went right in '54.

Herb Score — he was good but he wasn't rated as the best lefty in the league. Most people said Pierce and Ford were better than him.

The reason they were rated better was because they had been pitching a while.

Score set the rookie strikeout record and won 16 games, then he won 20 in his second year. How good would he have become?

I think that Herb Score could have been one of the greatest. He had everything. He had a terrific fastball, good curveball, and, for a fellow that threw *hard* like he did, he had good control. He was headed for some great years. I think he would have been one of the greatest we had here in Cleveland.

That ball that hit him in the eye really slowed him up a lot as far as his career was concerned, *but*, when he came back, he was throwing good again. Bobby Bragan was the manager of the Indians then and when Score came back to start pitching, we used him in batting practice a few times just to get him used to the hitters hitting the ball back through the mound.

Finally came the day that he started and he looked just as good as he did before. But, then, in a game shortly afterward, he pulled a muscle in his elbow and that's what changed his career around. He was throwing really good when he came back, but after he pulled that muscle in his elbow his pitching changed.

Later you took Cal McLish, who had been around forever with no success, and got a couple of real good years out of him. How?

Cal was a control pitcher. He pitched to spots and he had a pretty good curveball, but he had one fault with it: He'd try to cut it a little short. He'd drop his elbow instead of going out in front with it and he'd throw his curveball about 55 feet instead of 60 feet six inches. He'd drop his elbow and kind of force it. I got him to reach a little more out in front, to keep his arm up and his elbow up. He started throwing his curveball the right distance and that helped him considerably. He nearly won 20 games for us one year.

In the late '50s you had three young fellows: Gary Bell, Jim Grant, and Jim Perry.

Gary Bell. I really liked him. He had a good fastball, but it was difficult for him to learn how to throw a curveball. He just had a little flat curveball. If he could have improved that a little, he'd have been a lot better pitcher. He was still a good pitcher, though. He needed a little better curveball and he needed a change of pace, to slow up, to give the hitters a different pitch to look at once in a while. I was kind of disappointed in myself because I couldn't get to him on a curveball or a change of pace. He was willing, but he couldn't come up with them. He worked on it a lot.

Perry was a control pitcher, changed speeds. I didn't do too much with him other than talk to him about pitching. He had a good sneaky fastball and he changed speeds good. He picked these things up himself.

Mudcat Grant was another fellow like Gary Bell. He had good stuff, a good fastball. It was for me to teach him a curveball but then after he left here he came up with a hard curveball, not a big one but a sharp one. It was more like a big slider.

A couple of years later you got Dick Donovan, who had been a pretty good pitcher for several years. You got his only 20-win season out of him. Did you do anything for him?

Oh, no, not Dick. You couldn't do much for Dick outside of picking the right spots for him or giving him the right rest.

Are there any pitchers who you had over the years who were disappointments to you?

I remember one: Dick Rozek. He's a big executive with an appliance manufacturer out in Iowa now. I had him for a couple of years. When he started to warm up out in the bullpen, everybody would stop and watch him. He was throwing so good and hard. He developed a pretty curveball. We worked on his control and his change of pace. He was always one of these fellows where you were hoping he'd come overnight. But we just couldn't get him over the hump. He'd throw so good in the bullpen and we'd put him in a game and he'd either throw too hard or press a lot. He just pressed so much he couldn't throw natural, just couldn't let his natural ability take over. He was one of my biggest disappointments. Some of these guys who kid a lot and have fun, you think they're loose, but they're the worst sometimes. I always thought he was relaxed and loose in the bullpen, but as soon as he got in a game and started pitching to a hitter he was a changed man.

Did anybody surprise you, do better than you expected?

That's a tough one. Guys like Bearden — we never counted on him much. In fact, in the beginning of '48 he wasn't even pitching regularly.

Did you have souvenirs from your career?

I have a number of them, but in the '20s and '30s and '40s we didn't have too many. I never saved a uniform or anything like that. What I have mostly are photographs and write-ups. Mother kept a scrapbook and my wife kept one for me. I still have them.

Do you look back on them often?

Only when I have a request from somebody for something they're trying to find out. I have to go back to get the correct information.

I had a World Series ring that I gave to one grandson. And the All-Star bats they used to give us. And trophies and cups. I gave a lot of them to the kids.

All I have now are the scrapbooks and photographs. I don't have much of it out. I have an autographed picture of Bob Hope, he was a stockholder when Bill Veeck bought the Indians — I think maybe he still is.

Do you receive much fan mail?

I receive more now than I did when I was pitching. I never got any fan mail when I was pitching in the '30s, people didn't bother with that. Nobody even bothered to get autographs in the '30s.

Do you get a lot of requests for autographs?

Yeah, quite a few.

I sign all the time. I've done a couple of card shows, but I hate to charge for this. The ones I do they may charge admission, but there's no charge for autographs.

One of the biggest complaints is the player not looking up or speaking. I always try to talk to them a little.

Would you do it all again?

I think so. I enjoyed my life in baseball. We didn't make much money, but we didn't know any better.

You were one of the top handful of pitchers in the American League. What would you make today?

Well, judging from what Steinbrenner gave this guy Perez, a million six hundred thousand or something like that and he won nine games in 1989. I won 11 or more games 15 times and I won 15 games or more eight times, so I think I'd be in line to make some of that big money.

What was your top salary?

$18,000. I thought they were getting by pretty easy with me, then I found out what Lefty Gomez made. He pitched good ball for the Yankees for a number of years and he didn't make much over $20,000.

But it was a different situation in the '30s. People were begging and out of work during the Depression. When I'd go back to Omaha, some of my best friends were out pushing a rake or a shovel on the WPA, making about a dollar a day. And glad to get it.

Salaries will go up more, there's no doubt about it. It's hard to believe they're paying some guys three million a year. I remember back when Babe Ruth was making $85,000. When he made that everybody thought it was great—he was making more than the president of the United States.

In 1933 we received a letter from Billy Evans, our general manager, saying everybody was going to take a 10 percent. You had to take it or leave it.

Back to my original question: Do you belong in the Hall of Fame?

If you go by entire career, and judging by these other fellows who are already in there, and I don't begrudge them, I'd say yes. Now they're putting in players from the black leagues and they have no records on them. They're just trying to satisfy the people by doing this.

I have doubts if I'll make it. They (the Veterans Committee) don't talk too much about their voting, you know. I got some information from a friend that I got the 75 percent once, but a couple of others got more.

I think I should be in. In my own mind, I know my arm injury in '36 and the arm operation in '41 changed my career quite a bit. I think without these, in the last 11 years of my career I could have won 50 or so more ballgames. That would have put me up there with Ted Lyons.

But you can't go on what might have been, you have to judge on what was done. My All-Star and coaching records should count for something.

Today some guys are elected on their managerial record, like Lopez. There's no reason why somebody like Bucky Harris or Jimmy Dykes or Charlie Grimm shouldn't be mentioned just as much as some of these other guys.

By golly, Bucky Harris managed about 25 years and Jimmy Dykes had good years as a player and he managed about 20 years. And Charlie Grimm is overlooked all the time. He was a good ballplayer, his statistics are good and he managed a long time with the Cubs. He gave a lot to baseball and he's never mentioned.

All the time you read where Leo Durocher might get in. If Leo Durocher gets in and you don't give it to guys like Grimm and Dykes you're just going backwards.

The high-profile individual is more likely to get in. Durocher was high-profile, the others not as much. This is one of the problems with your career—you just went out and did your job.

That's what happened in New York when I pitched in the '34 All-Star

Game. I was pitching out here (Cleveland) without a lot of publicity, and the New York writers just wouldn't pay any attention to me. The next day a couple of them looked at the box score and saw I had pitched five innings of one-hit ball. They hardly knew who I was. Hubbell got all the publicity.

No one had a one-game or career All-Star record like you did.

Yes, but Gomez pitched good ball in the All-Star Games and Marichal had a good record.

* * *

Mel Harder makes a quiet disclaimer about his All-Star Game performance. Several pitchers have performed in several All-Star Games with great success, but none as well as Mel. Here is Mel's record compared to the records of the other top hurlers in All-Star competition (minimum nine innings in All-Star Games).

Pitcher, W-L	G	GS	IP	H	R	ER	BB	SO	ERA
Mel HARDER, 1-0	4	0	13	9	0	0	1	5	0.00
Juan Marichal, 2-0	8	2	18	7	2	1	2	12	0.50
Jim Bunning, 1-1	8	3	18	7	3	2	1	13	1.00
Lefty Gomez, 3-1	5	5	18	11	6	5	3	9	2.50
Carl Hubbell, 0-0	5	1	9.2	8	3	3	6	11	2.79

MELVIN LeROY (CHIEF, WIMPY) HARDER
Born October 15, 1909, Beemer, NE
Ht. 6'1" Wt. 195 Batted and Threw Right

Year	Team	G	IP	W	L	PCT	H	BB	SO	SHO	SV	ERA
1928	CleA	23	49	0	2	.000	64	32	15	0	1	6.61
1929		11	17.2	1	0	1.000	24	5	4	0	0	5.60
1930		36	175.1	11	10	.524	205	68	44	0	2	4.21
1931		40	194	13	14	.481	229	72	63	0	1	4.36
1932		39	254.2	15	13	.536	277	68	90	1	0	3.75
1933		43	253	15	17	.469	254	67	81	2	4	2.95
1934		44	255.1	20	12	.625	246	81	91	6*	4	2.61
1935		42	287.1	22	11	.667	313	53	95	4	2	3.29
1936		36	224.2	15	15	.500	294	71	84	0	1	5.17
1937		38	233.2	15	12	.556	268	86	95	0	2	4.28
1938		38	240	17	10	.630	257	62	102	2	4	3.83
1939		29	208	15	9	.615	213	64	67	1	1	3.50
1940		31	186.1	12	11	.522	200	59	76	0	0	4.06

Year	Team	G	IP	W	L	PCT	H	BB	SO	SHO	SV	ERA
1941		15	68.2	5	4	.556	76	37	21	0	1	5.24
1942		29	198.2	13	14	.481	179	82	74	4	0	3.44
1943		19	135.1	8	7	.533	126	61	40	1	0	3.06
1944		30	196.1	12	10	.545	211	69	64	2	0	3.71
1945		11	76	3	7	.300	93	23	16	0	0	3.67
1946		13	92.1	5	4	.556	85	31	21	1	0	3.41
1947		15	80	6	4	.600	91	27	17	1	0	4.50
20 years		582	3426.1	223	186	.545	3706	1118	1160	25	23	3.80

*Led league

All-Star Game

Year	League		ST	IP	H	R	ER	BB	SO	ERA
1934	American	(w)		5	1	0	0	1	2	0.00
1935				3	1	0	0	0	1	0.00
1936				2	2	0	0	0	2	0.00
1937				3	5	0	0	0	0	0.00
4 years		(1-0)	0	13	9	0	0	1	5	0.00

SID HUDSON

Sid Hudson (George Brace photograph).

Second Division
AL All-Star 1941, 1942

> "Joe DiMaggio ... said there wasn't a pitcher on the Brooklyn staff that showed him as much stuff as I did."
> — Sid Hudson

When the Washington Senators won on Opening Day, 1950, it marked the first time the team had been in first place since Opening Day of 1945. Each time, though, they lost on Day 2 and the pennant race in our nation's capital was over for another year.

Since their last American League pennant in 1933, other than two wartime second-place finishes, the team had finished over .500 only once.

The Senators had had a few stars over that period: Buddy Myer, Cecil Travis, Dutch Leonard, Mickey Vernon, George Case, Eddie Yost, Doc Cramer, Bobo Newsom, Eddie Robinson, Sid Hudson, Walt Masterson.

But there never seemed to be a supporting cast and the stars couldn't do it alone, so the Senators continued to be also-rans. After a fourth-place finish (76–78) in 1946, the team never entered the first division again. In 1960, though, the misery ended: The Griffith family moved the club to the Twin Cities.

Nineteen fifty was the tenth anniversary of Sid Hudson's rookie year, when he made the ultimate baseball jump — from Class D to the major leagues. World War II had cost him three years, so it was only his eighth season — and probably his best, considering his surroundings.

Yost was there in '50, and Vernon rejoined the club in June after a season-plus in Cleveland, but sprinkled throughout the lineup were such names as Al Evans, Bud Stewart, Cass Michaels, Mickey Grasso, etc. Assisting Hudson on the mound was a pitching staff made up of names today's fans have never heard of: Al Sima, Elmer Singleton, Mickey Harris, Connie Marrero, Joe Haynes, etc.

Sid had won 17 as a rookie in 1940 and was selected for the All-Star Game in both '41 and '42, but on those Washington teams were Travis, Case, Vernon, Rick Ferrell, Stan Spence, Newsom, Leonard, Gee Walker, Cramer, and a few others who were recognizable names and legitimate big league players.

But 1950's squad was manned mostly with has-beens or never-would-be's. Mostly the latter. In the eight-team AL, Washington was seventh in batting, seventh in fielding, and sixth in pitching.

Sid shone in 1950. He won 14 games; no other Senator pitcher won more than eight. He led the team in starts, complete games, and innings.

Today, Sid Hudson is still associated with baseball after a half century. He's the pitching coach for Baylor University.

You pitched two years in Class D and then jumped to the majors and hardly skipped a beat. How did the Senators acquire you?

Sid Hudson: They purchased me. A cash purchase — me and another pitcher by the name of (Harry) Dean. He called himself "Dizzy."

You had been owned by the Sanford (Florida State League) club?

Yes. They were independently owned then.

How did Sanford acquire you?

I got a call from the manager at Sanford, Florida, in Chattanooga, Tennessee, where I lived. He had seen me play some in semi-pro ball — he lived in Cleveland, Tennessee. I was a first baseman and he said he needed a first baseman, so I went to Sanford and played first base for about two weeks and did pretty well, but we had a losing record and we changed managers. The new manager came — Raw Meat Rodgers. He was quite famous in baseball. He was a player, an owner, a manager, a general manager, scout — the whole works. He brought a first baseman with him so now I'm sitting on the bench.

After he'd been there about a week, we were playing in Palatka, Florida, and we were getting beat pretty bad. In the eighth inning he said to me, "Have you ever pitched any?" I said, "Yeah." He said, "Well, you've got a good arm. You've got the next two innings." I struck out the side in both innings. He said, "From now on, you're gonna be a pitcher."

So one day I'd pitch, the next day I'd play first base, the next day third base, the next day outfield, then I'd pitch again. We finished on the bottom that year and I won 11 and lost seven. (With an ERA of 2.02.)

The next year we had a new manager and some new players and we won the pennant. I won 24 and lost four (1.79 ERA) and then I won four more games in the playoffs. That year I started 31 games and finished 31. I think that was a record for a long time, may still be. Then I was sold to Washington.

You had a great rookie year in 1940 (17-16 for a 64-90 team). That year the Chicago chapter of the BBWAA began the first Rookie of the Year award and continued it through 1946, when the present award was inaugurated.

Lou Boudreau beat me out by three votes, but he had played about 30 games the year before. (In 1939, Boudreau appeared in 53 games and had 225 at bats with a .258 average. Under ROY rules for any other year he would have been ineligible for the award.)

You were chosen for the All-Star Game in both '41 and '42. Arky Vaughan homered off of you in the '41 game.

SH: We were ahead 2-to-1 going into the seventh inning, and I went in to pitch. I was supposed to pitch the seventh, eighth, and ninth. First batter up, Enos Slaughter, a left-handed hitter, hit a little dinker back of third base for a double. The next batter bunted him to third and that brought up Arky Vaughan and he hit a home run. Then I got the next two batters out. It was my turn to hit, so they sent in a pinch-hitter for me.

You were a good hitter.

I enjoyed trying to hit anyway. I pinch-hit a few times with Washington.

After '42, you spent three years in the service. Did you play ball?

Yes, but I hurt my arm while I was in the service. I was stationed in

Sid Hudson (courtesy of *The National Pastime*).

Waco, Texas, at an Army air field and I pitched 220-and-some-odd innings that year.

I was in the Special Services and I gave calisthenics to cadets about five times a day, five days a week. Pitching that much and all that exercise, the doctor told me I developed a spur on my shoulder and it was caused from the excessive activity. I was never quite the same after that.

The doctor in Johns Hopkins in Baltimore — Dr. Bennett was the Jobe of his day (Dr. Frank Jobe, the orthopedist who developed the Tommy John elbow surgical procedure) — told me I was through unless I could find some other position to throw from. I was a three-quarter arm pitcher. He said maybe I could drop down and get away from the pain. I was able to sidearm hitters before that, but I started to throwing every pitch sidearm for the last seven or eight years I pitched in the big leagues. He told me he could operate and take it (the spur) off. He said, "Of course, if I cut on your shoulder, that doesn't mean you're really going to be all right." I said, "Let's try the other first."

Nature kind of took care of it. I had it X-rayed a couple years later and it was gone. It bothered me a little bit in the spring but it would came around and I was okay. Once in a while I'd act like I was coming sidearm, then I'd throw overhand. Get a left-handed hitter up there, it was kind of a surprise action. It did get a lot better. It had to — I continued to pitch quite a while.

You were never on a winning team until the end of your career.

In Boston we won a little. I think we finished fourth in Washington one year. That was the best we ever finished while I was there.

Did you ever wonder what you might have accomplished if you had played for a better club?

Phi Rizzuto told me in 1941 that I was gonna be a Yankee the next season and, sure enough, they tried to deal for me but Mr. Griff (Senators owner Clark Griffith) wouldn't part with me. I was hoping that would happen. (Laughs)

When I first joined them, the knuckle ball pitchers were all there, like Dutch Leonard, Roger Wolff, John Niggeling, and Mickey Haefner — they had four of 'em. They had some young pitchers and they didn't develop like they thought they would. I was the only one who didn't throw a knuckleball and the catcher was always glad to see me pitch. (Laughs)

In '45, the Senators made a run at the pennant, but you and Walt Masterson and Early Wynn and several others were in the service. You guys could have made the difference.

Oh, yes.

On Babe Ruth Day at Yankee Stadium in 1947 you pitched against the Yankees.

I was kind of sorry to see Babe Ruth in that condition at that time. I pitched that day and beat 'em, one-to-nothing. I got a base hit in the seventh inning and they sacrificed me to second and Buddy Lewis got a single and I scored the run. That was against Spud Chandler.

Was that your best game?

Not at all. One of the best games I ever pitched and the biggest thrill I ever had was against Lefty Grove (of) Boston. He was my idol as a youngster growing up and I faced him one Sunday afternoon in Washington and I beat him one-to-nothing in 13 innings.

I had a no-hitter going in to the ninth inning against the Browns. We were ahead one-to-nothing going in to the ninth. First batter up, Rip Radcliff, hit a line drive down the right field line and it hit the chalk line for a double. George McQuinn was the next hitter and he tried to bunt the ball. He bunted at it and missed it and my catcher missed it and the runner goes to third.

Now I've got a runner on third and no outs and a one-run lead. So I struck McQuinn out, Harlond Clift popped up, and Walt Judnich popped up. So I got a one-hitter.

The Browns had some good hitters but always lacked pitching.
They had some excellent hitters back then.
Harlond Clift was certainly an underrated player.
Yes, he was. He was a good hitter.
Who was the best player you saw?
Joe DiMaggio. He could do it all.
Who was the toughest batter for you?

I'd say for about a three-year stretch, Larry Doby. He hit me good for about three years, then he kind of turned it around. I got him out after that. He just hit shots off me all the time for about three years.

He was a pretty good hitter. He had power. He hit a home run off of me in Washington over the right field scoreboard. The scoreboard was about 340 feet and was big and tall and on top of that was a Chesterfield cigarette sign. It was really high. He hit it over that. The last time I saw it, it disappeared into the night.

It ended up I won the game. The next day I came to the ballpark and in old Griffith Stadium the office was in front and you had to walk right by it. Mr. Griffith was in his office upstairs and he saw me from his window and he said, "Hey, come up here. I want to talk to you."

I went up there and first thing he said to me — he called everybody "Young Man"— was, "Young Man, you ought to ashamed to let that n----- hit a ball that far off of you." (Laughs)

A couple of your teammates in Washington were excellent ball players. Mickey Vernon — a lot of people say he should be in the Hall of Fame.

I think so, too. On top of that, he's a fine gentleman. In fact, we keep in close touch with each other.

What about Eddie Yost?
Oh, great! Great!
If he'd have played on a team with post-season exposure and TV and all, he would have been raved about.

He was one of the best third basemen in the league and he had quite an eye at the plate and he was a pretty good hitter. They called him "The Walking Man." Quite a guy, too.

Hall of Fame?
Oh, sure. I think there's some in there that don't deserve it like he does.
Was there a team that you either had trouble with or an easy time with?
The Yankees beat me a lot of times, but I pitched a lot of games against them. I think I won about 18 or 19 games against 'em, but I lost quite a few, too. It seems like I pitched against 'em every time they came to town or we went up there.

Detroit and Cleveland I pitched good against, Chicago was just so-so, Browns pretty good, but I lost a lot more games than I won. There were some good players back in those days.

Who was the best pitcher you saw?

For the best stuff of any pitcher I ever saw, it was Bob Feller. I thought he threw the hardest of any pitcher I ever saw and any pitcher I've ever seen since, and that includes Nolan Ryan.

Feller lost four years in the service right in his prime and he still had nearly 3,000 strikeouts and he'd have probably won a hundred more games. He was the toughest pitcher I ever saw. I know I hit at him quite a few times. I got some hits off of him, but he could really throw.

One day we were playing Cleveland and we were behind a run going into the ninth inning and we got the bases loaded and no outs. Feller was down in the bullpen throwing — he was just warming up for his next game. But they brought him in the game. We had the meat of our lineup — Ben Chapman and GeeGee Walker and I think Mickey Vernon.

GeeGee was the first hitter and he threw him three fastballs and he stood there and never took the bat off his shoulder. Chapman went up and he did the same thing. He came back to the bench and said, "I didn't see 'em."

By this time, Bucky Harris, the manager, said, "You think he's pretty quick today, huh?" They all said they didn't see him. He said, "If you think he's quick, you should have been Walter Johnson in *his* prime. Then Grove, then Feller." Anyway, Feller struck out all three in a row. (Laughs)

You were traded to Boston in 1952. You had been with Washington a long time; how did you feel about the trade?

I hated to leave Washington. After all, you leave all your buddies and everything, but I was kind of glad to get a chance to maybe pitch for a better club.

I enjoyed my stay in Boston. I really did. First of all, it was much cooler. Washington, D.C., was pretty humid. My family liked it in Boston, too.

When you retired as an active player, you stayed in the game for a long, long time.

Boston turned me loose after the 1955 spring training and offered me a job scouting and I took it. I scouted for them for about six years.

Then they formed the new Washington Senators and Mickey Vernon was the manager so I went back as his pitching coach. Then I was a big league coach for about a dozen years for six or eight managers. I coached some for Gil Hodges and Whitey Herzog and Billy Martin, Jim Lemon, Frank Lucchesi, Bill Hunter. Then I was a minor league pitching coach for Washington and Texas.

I was a big league pitching coach through 1978 with Texas and then I started scouting again for Texas in the states of Texas and New Mexico. In the summers, I would go to Sarasota, Florida, and work with all the new signees — the pitchers. I did that through 1986 and then I retired.

Now I'm pitching coach for Baylor University and have been since I left Texas. I've enjoyed good health so I'm still pretty active.

You've been associated with baseball for more than 50 years and there have been a lot of changes in the game. What's the biggest one?

Of course, money is the biggest one.

The fields are a little better than they were in my day. The balls and bats seem to be the same. They claim the ball's pretty lively today, but we had some lively balls in our day, and some dead ones, too. The uniforms are different.

I think the biggest change is relief pitching. It's taking over. Starters are geared to go five or six or seven innings and I don't care what the score is, they always taken 'em out. If a guy has a shutout going, somebody comes in and pitches the ninth inning. It's all relievers. The game doesn't start until about the seventh inning, then the relievers take over.

We used to be proud to pitch a full nine inning game, but it's not that today. Now they don't care.

You mentioned the field conditions. People today rave about Ryne Sandberg and Ozzie Smith, but what could guys like Lou Boudreau and Marty Marion have done on fields like they have today?

Oh, my goodness. They'd have never missed one. And Rizzuto and (Mark) Belanger and (Luis) Aparicio. They could get that ball then.

Astroturf is a big change, of course. It's a different ball game on Astroturf. Really and truly, it's not a real, *true* baseball game on Astroturf.

Going in to Kansas City when we played there when I was coaching, the pitchers wouldn't run on it. It bothered their legs. And I'd rather see a game on regular turf than Astroturf.

Did you save souvenirs?

Yes, I have quite a few. I have a ball signed by Harry Truman and Eisenhower and Ford and Nixon. I have a bushel basket full of autographed balls — all teams. I have Dizzy Dean and all those.

I have a scrapbook that has a leather cover on it. It has baseballs tooled in each corner and my glove and name on it. I took that and had all the players sign it in ink. Then I took an electric needle and traced over each name. And I have Ryan and Aaron and DiMaggio and Williams and Hornsby and Berra and Feller and all the old Hall of Famers. It's quite a piece.

I have a lot of souvenirs in what I call my Baseball Room. (Laughs)

Do you get much fan mail?

Yes, I do. I continue to get it — three or four letters a week. Autographs. Kids say, "I'm sorry I didn't get to see you pitch, but my grandpa did." (Laughs)

Would you go back and do it all again?

Sure. I'd love to. I enjoyed it. I really did.

Do you have any regrets?

Yes. If I had it to do over again, I think I'd work a little harder in the winter. I'd throw and really work at it.

I enjoyed my career. It's exactly what I wanted to do as a youngster and that's all I ever thought of. It came true, but I should have been better than what I was.

I look back at the better hitters — DiMaggio and Williams and all those guys — and I got those guys out pretty decent. I think I really concentrated and was bearing down more on them than on some of the mediocre hitters.

In 1941 the Yankees won the pennant and beat Brooklyn in the World Series. I pitched the last game of the season in Yankee Stadium against 'em and shut 'em out. After the World Series was over, I found a little quote in the paper by Joe DiMaggio. he said there wasn't a pitcher on the Brooklyn staff that showed him as much stuff as I did the last game of the season. I thought that was quite a compliment coming from him. That's in my scrapbook.

* * *

We touched on Sid's hitting up there. He had a .220 average for 12 years and in 1946 and '47 he teamed with Early Wynn to give the Senators one of the best 1-2 punches in baseball from the ninth spot in the batting order.

In '46, the first year back from the war for both men, Wynn batted .319 and Hudson .279. Then in '47, Sid shot up to .308 while Early held tough at .275. The combined two-year average for the two hurlers was .289. The Senators' average for those two seasons was .251.

* * *

Pitching was never the strong point of the original Senators and over the years very few of the team's hurlers were selected for the All-Star Game. Here is the complete list.

Wes Ferrell — 1937
Dutch Leonard — 1940, '43, '44
SID HUDSON — 1941, '42
Walt Masterson — 1947, '48
Early Wynn — 1947

Connie Marrero — 1951
Bob Porterfield — 1954
Dean Stone — 1954
Pedro Ramos — 1959

SIDNEY CHARLES HUDSON
Born January 3, 1917, Coalfield, TN
Ht. 6'4"   Wt. 180   Batted and Threw Right

Year	Team	G	IP	W	L	PCT	H	BB	SO	SHO	SV	ERA
1940	WasA	38	252	17	16	.515	272	81	96	3	1	4.57
1941		33	249.2	13	14	.481	242	97	108	3	0	3.46
1942		35	239.1	10	17	.370	266	70	72	1	2	4.36
1946		31	142.1	8	11	.421	160	37	35	1	1	3.60

Year	Team	G	IP	W	L	PCT	H	BB	SO	SHO	SV	ERA
1947	WasA	20	106	6	9	.400	113	58	37	1	0	5.60
1948		39	182	4	16	.200	217	107	53	0	1	5.88
1949		40	209	8	17*	.320	234	91	54	2	1	4.22
1950		30	237.2	14	14	.500	261	98	75	0	0	4.09
1951		23	138.2	5	12	.294	168	52	43	0	0	5.13
1952	WasA	7	62.2	3	4	.429	59	29	24	0	0	2.73
	BosA	21	134.1	7	9	.438	145	36	50	0	0	3.62
	Year	28	197	10	13	.435	204	65	74	0	0	3.34
1953	BosA	30	156	6	9	.400	164	49	60	0	2	3.52
1954		33	71.1	3	4	.429	83	30	27	0	5	4.42
12 years		380	2181	104	152	.406	2384	835	734	11	13	4.28

*Led league

All-Star Game

Year	League	ST	IP	H	R	ER	BB	SO	ERA
1941	American		1	3	2	2	1	1	18.00
1942			Selected, did not play						

WILLARD MARSHALL

Willard Marshall (George Brace photograph).

Old Country Boy
NL All-Star 1942, 1947, 1949

"I had a pretty good career for an old country boy."
— Willard Marshall

In 1951, Willard Marshall, the regular right fielder for the Boston Braves, fielded 1.000.

Many of the readers under the age of 40 probably aren't too impressed by that, for a couple of reasons. One, it's done on a fairly regular basis today — seven times in the '80s an outfielder played over 100 games in a season without an error. In 1982 alone, four did it. And two, fielding prowess today, with a few exceptions, is ignored. Sure, Ozzie Smith gets a lot of press (and money) and Ryne Sandberg is a robot with the glove and there are Gold Glove awards, but does anyone care?

Baseball cards used to give us fielding stats on the backs, but no more.

Granted, they (fielding stats) leave a great deal unexplained and not considered. A base hit to the outfield, for instance, which an outfielder picks up cleanly and rifles home, holding a runner on third and preventing him from scoring, counts *nothing* for the outfielder. If, however, the ball gets by him or he throws it over the catcher's head, then he gets acknowledgment, to wit: an error. Ditto the infielder who makes a brilliant play on a ball up the middle, saving a run. The batter gets a hit, of course, but the infielder receives nothing positive. Only if he throws the ball away can he affect his fielding average.

Those same two balls, the hit to the outfield and the grounder up the middle, can have very different results if the outfielder throws to the wrong base or the infielder doesn't get a glove on the ball. In both cases, the run scores. In neither case is the fielder's average affected. The guys in the paragraph above both did better jobs and somehow this should be able to be seen statistically. No game lends itself better to numbers. Someone should be able to devise some method whereby fielding ability can be recognized.

But kids today don't care about fielding. Their Sunday papers have batting and pitching stats every week, but where are the fielding stats, inconclusive though they be? Even *The Sporting News*— the Bible — gives us fielding averages only rarely, if that. Once upon a time, long, long ago, in a galaxy not so far away, fielding was considered more important than hitting. Check the nineteenth-century guides.

And fielding is being more de-emphasized daily. College coaches and scouts come around to high school coaches and ask, "Do you have anyone who can hit the ball?" or "Any live arms on the team?" They don't ever ask, "Do you have anyone who can recognize a ground ball when he sees it?" or "Is there anyone on the team who knows the difference between a pop fly and a house fly?"

So fielding inefficiency is being propagated at all levels.

But, comes the roar, fielding averages are improving every year! Of course they are. With the size of the gloves today and the elimination of bad (or even uneven) bounces with carpeting (the natural surfaces are also better kept and smoother than ever in the past), it becomes an increasing challenge *not* to field a ball cleanly.

But what happens after the ball is beaten into submission? Since the average player does not know what to do with the ball, it is not reasonable to expect the average fan to know what he's supposed to do with it, either. Someday, if you have the good fortune, watch a ballgame with an old-time player. Have him tell you what's going wrong. Outfielders throwing to the wrong bases, infielders forcing throws that shouldn't be made. This is fielding and this is where the great game is lacking.

Okay, now we will return to the subject at hand: Willard Marshall.

As pointed out above, Willard fielded 1.000 in 1951. At that time, it had been done only once before in the entire history of the game, by Danny Litwhiler of the Phillies in 1942. The table on page 77 lists all the perfect fielding outfielders, chronologically, through 1970, after which it has occurred frequently.

Note that Marshall and Litwhiler were the only ones to accomplish it prior to 1962. By that year, expansion had begun and, with it, artificial playing surfaces had started to spring up. This was also the time that gloves began to grow. Paul Richards (actually, his coach, Al Vincent) created the over-sized catcher's mitt in the late '50s so Gus Triandos could better handle Hoyt Wilhelm's knuckler, and within a very few years the idea of excessively-sized leather arm extensions for everyone caught on. So in the early '60s, stopping the ball started becoming easier for everyone.

But back in '51, the gloves weren't so big and the fields weren't so smooth. And Willard Marshall was a good fielder. He began as a center fielder, but he was not fast and his strong arm was better suited to right. When he was moved over there in 1947 he became one of the best right fielders in the National League. In seven years as a regular right fielder, he led the league twice each in assists and double plays and once in average. Another season he made only one miscue and finished second in fielding by .00082.

Willard is retired today and loving it. Although he lives up north now, he retains the slow southern drawl of his upbringing in Virginia.

You signed originally with the Atlanta Crackers. That was a good brand of baseball in those days and you stepped right into the lineup at 19. How did the Giants acquire you?

Willard Marshall: Originally when I left Atlanta I was going to go to the Brooklyn Dodgers. They were trying to buy me, but with the war coming on they changed their minds and decided they wouldn't take me. Then the Giants stepped in and they took me.

You really impressed Mel Ott (Giants manager) in spring training in 1942.

Oh, yeah. I had a *very* good spring training with the Giants. Couldn't have done any better.

You were selected for the All-Star Game as a rookie.

Yes, I was. It was certainly a big thrill.

How were you doing at the All-Star break?

I don't remember now. The year started out very good, but it didn't last the whole year. I kind of tapered off, but at the All-Star Game I guess I was doing fairly good.

In '43 you entered the Marine Corps. Draft or enlist?

I enlisted.

Did you play ball in the Marines?

A little bit. Not too much.

You returned to the Giants in '46 and stepped right back in the starting lineup, then in '47 the team set a home run record. Almost all the players on the team had their best home run year ever. Why?

I wish I could tell you why. I don't know. It was just one of those years when everybody was hitting home runs. I don't know why.

Do you remember any particular home run that season?

The only thing I can remember outstanding was three home runs in one ballgame. I think it was against Cincinnati. I don't remember the pitchers.

And there were other good games but after the years you don't remember them.

That was the only season I hit over 20 home runs. I could never figure out why I never did it again.

The Giants traded you after the '49 season in a trade that probably brought them the '51 pennant (Marshall, Sid Gordon, Buddy Kerr, and Red Webb for Alvin Dark and Eddie Stanky). How did you feel?

Well, I don't know. I guess when you play baseball you feel it could come at any time. It doesn't bother you too much. Once you move, you get used to it. Baseball is baseball, regardless of where you are. I hated to leave, but there was nothing I could do about it.

How did you like playing in Boston?

I enjoyed it. Boston's a good town. The Braves didn't draw too good a crowd.

In 1951 with the Braves you became the second outfielder ever to go a full season without making an error.

Yes. The first was Danny Litwhiler.

You were a right fielder and you had a reputation of being a little slow-footed but having a heck of a strong arm and very sure hands.

I always said if I could get to it, I could catch it. I could hold on to it. I was always noted for having a good arm.

Did you ever play anywhere but the outfield?

They tried me when I was ending at third and at first. Paul Richards did when I was with the White Sox.

Willard Marshall (courtesy of *The National Pastime*).

Is there any game in your career that stands out in your memory?

Well, not particularly. Of course, there's the All-Star Games (Willard played in three, '42, '47, and '49) and the first ballgame you play when you go the majors. They're very special. I remember being very excited in my first fame.

Who was the best overall player you saw?

A guy I was always very enthused with and always admired very much was Stan Musial.

I would say for four or five years, probably the *best* ballplayer, in my opinion, was (Jackie) Robinson. I don't think there was anybody any better than him for four or five years.

What were the feelings on the Giants at that time toward him?

There were some that just would not accept it, but some of that's still around today. But he sure put up with it.

On the Giants, it wasn't too bad. There were a couple of southerners. I was a southerner, myself, but I never felt the way some of them did. There were two or three of them, even some on Brooklyn, who had things to say.

Who was the best pitcher you saw?

For me, left-handed, I'd have to take Warren Spahn, I guess. And right-handed, Carl Erskine from the Dodgers.

Was there any pitcher who was particularly easy for you?

None of them were *easy*, but I guess I hit (Ewell) Blackwell with Cincinnati as well as anybody. He was tough on the right-handers, there's no question about it.

What's the major change in baseball over the last 50 years?

Well, everything has changed, not only baseball. Everything in baseball has changed somewhat, but it's still baseball and still played the same way.

You ended up in the American League your last two years. If you were there today, you'd probably be a DH. What do you think of the DH?

I prefer it the other way—without the DH. I think it takes something away from the game. The game wasn't meant to be played that way. I think it's better the way we had it—the pitcher had to hit.

The managers don't have to maneuver the players. With the pitcher coming up, you had to do a little more thinking out there.

Did you collect souvenirs from your career?

Not too much. I have some bats and balls and gloves and old stuff that I had during my playing career.

In fact, I just got an old glove—I was looking for it for a long time and my father-in-law found it—that I think was the same glove I used when I fielded the thousand.

I was invited down to Portsmouth, Virginia, and they inducted me into the Virginia Hall of Fame. At that time, they asked me if I had a bat or a glove or uniform or something they could put in that museum. I'm going to send it (the glove) down to Portsmouth, I think, along with my old Giants uniform and a bat. I had never been there to the museum myself and I was very impressed. My wife still talks about it.

In fact, there are two or three museums there. I went through the Navy museum—they've got a lot of interesting stuff right along there together.

What did you do when you left baseball?

I was scouting with the Giants for a while and then I went to work in the real estate business with my father-in-law. Then I went to work for the town of Fort Lee (New Jersey) and worked for them for 25 years. Now I'm retired.

How do you like it?

Very much. I'm enjoying every minute.

Did you sign anybody of note when you were a scout?

The only one that I signed I thought was going to go all the way was John Orsino, the catcher. I thought he was going to make it. Kind of a hot-headed kid, I think that ruined him. But he looked good at the time.

Do you get much fan mail today?

I guess I average about one a day. There's more today than there was a few years ago.

They're requests for autographs. I understand a lot of fellows around won't sign. I don't understand that. Guys making more money today than they ever did in their life and they won't sign an autograph.

I was told, "Well, you should get paid to sign your autograph," and I said, "What the heck. Are you kidding me?" When I get 'em, I sign 'em and send 'em back.

Did you get many autograph requests when you were active?

Yeah. You could sit down and write all day if you wanted to. I didn't pass up many chances. If I had a chance to sign 'em, I signed 'em. There were times, though, when you had things you had to do — you couldn't stop and sit down with 'em. But I always liked to give the kids whatever they wanted.

There wasn't as much of it then as there is now. It's strictly business now. When you go to those card shows, you can't believe what goes on. They bring guys like (Johnny) Mize and those guys around here and give him like $2,500 and all that foolishness. It's almost unbelievable.

A while back, they had Bobby Thomson and Don Mueller and myself and Sal Yvars together and they had pictures there that they were getting 20 bucks for. I could see it with Bobby Thomson, maybe, but not for me or some of those. But they were nice pictures.

I think that's obscene — it's crazy — to ask a kid for money like that. But today, the fathers don't seem to mind shelling it out for these kids.

For me to ask a guy to give me five dollars to sign an autograph — I could never do that.

What was your top salary?

Oh, I think my top salary was around 20-some thousand. With the Braves.

Today everything's gone crazy — with TV and all. How in the world can you picture a guy making $4 million a year playing baseball? He's coming along at a great time in his young life. What's scary about it is the rate it's going, it's going to get worse. But it's not just baseball, it's everything.

If you went back 50 years, would you do it all again?

I certainly would.

Is there anything you'd do differently?

I don't know. I don't think so. What could you do differently, except play the game the best you know how and try to be a nice guy and try to be sociable?

Play the game. Enjoy it. And I enjoyed every minute of it.
I had a pretty good career for an old country boy.

* * *

Let's take a quick look at the 1947 Giants. They hit home runs at a previously unimagined pace. In a 154-game schedule, only the 1956 Cincinnati Reds matched them and only three times in a 162-game schedule has their total of 221 been surpassed. The table at top of page 78 shows the teams with the ten highest single season home run totals, listed chronologically, through 1995.

In over four decades, even with an expanded schedule, the record did not go up much, less than 9 percent. In fact, the 221 is still the National League record. Since the Reds in '56, the best in the Senior Circuit has been 209 by the Cubs in 1987.

Prior to '47, the Yankees of 1936 held the team home run mark with 182 and the '30 Cubs held the NL record with 171, so the 221 hit by the Giants blew away the old standards: a 21 percent increase over the previous major league record and a whopping 29 percent hike above the old league mark.

An accomplishment of this magnitude requires a total team effort, and that's what the Giants had. Of their starting eight, seven hit more home runs than they ever had before and five had the biggest single season of their entire careers, before *or* after. The one regular, Buddy Kerr, who had a previous higher total, had his second-best total. Twenty-five homers came from men who had never before hit a major league home run. Fifteen came from men who would never hit another major league home run. Seven were from men who had never hit a home run before and would never hit one again. The table at bottom of page 78 shows the 1947 New York Giants' home runs.

The record-setter, number 183, was hit by Jack "Lucky" Lohrke, a rookie whose at-bats, hits, and RBI's decreased each season of his seven-year career. (Lohrke's nickname was acquired when he was called up to Triple-A from Spokane of the old Western International League. He got the call just minutes before the Spokane team bus pulled out for a road trip. A few miles down the road, the bus crashed, killing several players.)

Lloyd Gearhart contributed six home runs to the record-breaking cause. It was the only major league season for the reserve outfielder/pinch-hitter and he was on the team only because Whitey Lockman broke his ankle and missed all but the last week of the season.

We can add one more distinction to Willard Marshall's super season. He became one of only 11 men in history to hit more than 35 home runs (36) and strike out fewer times (30). (See the table at the end of Andy Pafko's chapter.)

It was a memorable year.

1.000 FA, OUTFIELDERS, 100 OR MORE GAMES, CHRONOLOGICALLY, THROUGH 1970

Year	Player, Team	G	PO	A	TC/G
1942	Danny Litwhiler, Philadelphia (NL)	151	308	9	2.1
1951	WILLARD MARSHALL, Boston (NL)	127	220	11	1.8
1962	Tony Gonzales, Philadelphia	114	268	8	2.4
1963	Don Demeter, Philadelphia	119	201	4	1.7
1965	Rocky Colavito, Cleveland	162	265	9	1.7
	Russ Snyder, Baltimore	106	188	4	1.8
1966	Curt Flood, St. Louis	159	391	5	2.5
1968	Ken Harrelson, Boston	132	241	8	1.9
	Mickey Stanley, Detroit	130	297	7	2.3
	Johnny Callison, Philadelphia	109	187	10	1.8
1969	Ken Berry, Chicago (AL)	120	215	7	1.9
1970	Mickey Stanley, Detroit	132	317	3	2.4

10 HIGHEST SINGLE-SEASON TEAM HOME RUN TOTALS, THROUGH 1995, LISTED CHRONOLOGICALLY

Year	Team, league	G	HR	HR/G
1947	New York, NL	155	221	1.43
1956	Cincinnati, NL	155	221	1.43
1961	New York, AL	163	240	1.47
1963	Minnesota, AL	161	225	1.40
1964	Minnesota, AL	163	221	1.36
1977	Boston, AL	161	213	1.323
1982	Milwaukee, AL	163	216	1.325
1985	Baltimore, AL	161	214	1.329
1987	Detroit, AL	162	225	1.39
1987	Toronto, AL	162	215	1.327

1947 NEW YORK GIANTS' HOME RUNS

Player, Pos	Home Runs	Best Previous Season	Best Succeeding Season
Johnny Mize, 1B	51	43	40
WILLARD MARSHALL, RF	36	13	17
Walker Cooper, C	35	13	20
*Bobby Thomson, CF	29	2	32
Bill Rigney, 2B-3B-SS	17	3	10
Sid Gordon, LF	13	9	30
*Jack Lohrke, 3B	11	-	5
Buddy Kerr, SS	7	9	2
*Lloyd Gearhart, OF	6	-	-
Ernie Lombardi, C	4	20	-
*Clint Hartung, P-OF	4	-	4
Mickey Witek, 2B	3	6	0
*Joe Lafata, OF	2	-	3
*Bobby Rhawn, INF	1	-	1
Ray Poat, P	1	0	0
Mort Cooper, P	1	2	0

Rookie

WILLARD WARREN MARSHALL
Born February 8, 1921, Richmond, VA
Ht. 6'1"   Wt. 205   Batted Left Threw Right

Year	Team	G	AB	R	H	2B	3B	HR	RBI	SB	BA	SA
1942	NYN	116	401	41	103	9	2	11	59	1	.257	.372
1946		131	510	63	144	18	3	13	48	3	.282	.406
1947		155*	587	102	171	19	6	36	107	3	.291	.528
1948		143	537	72	146	21	8	14	86	2	.272	.419
1949		141	499	81	153	19	3	12	70	4	.307	.429
1950	BosN	105	298	38	70	10	2	5	40	1	.235	.332
1951		136	469	65	132	24	7	11	62	0	.281	.433
1952	BosN	21	66	5	15	4	1	2	11	0	.227	.409
	CinN	107	397	52	106	23	1	8	46	0	.267	.390
	Year	128	463	57	121	27	2	10	57	0	.261	.393
1953	CinN	122	357	51	95	14	6	17	62	0	.266	.482

Year	Team	G	AB	R	H	2B	3B	HR	RBI	SB	BA	SA
1954	ChiA	47	71	7	18	2	0	1	7	0	.254	.324
1955	ChiA	22	41	6	7	0	0	0	6	0	.171	.171
11 years		1246	4233	583	1160	163	39	130	604	14	.274	.423

*Led league

All-Star Game

Year	League	G	AB	R	H	2B	3B	HR	RBI	SB	BA	SA
1942	National	1	1	0	0	0	0	0	0	0	.000	.000
1947		1	1	0	0	0	0	0	0	0	.000	.000
1949		1	1	1	0	0	0	0	0	0	.000	.000
3 years		3	3	1	0	0	0	0	0	0	.000	.000

JOE MOORE

Joe Moore (George Brace photograph).

Team Player
NL All-Star 1935, 1936, 1937, 1938, 1940

"We didn't get rich like they are now, but we had a whole lot more fun."

— Joe Moore

Joe Moore had an excellent major league career, one that most men would love to brag about, but in the interview with him which follows it is apparent that the team was far more important to him than any personal achievement. Even when asked if there was one game which stood out, he talked of a team accomplishment rather than something he did himself.

There are several team-related records of which Joe is a part:

He played on one World Championship club (1933) and three NL pennant winners (1933, '36, '37).

In 1935, he teamed with Bill Terry and Hank Leiber to give the Giants three men with over 200 hits. Only the 1929 Phillies and, later, the 1937 Tigers had more (4).

On July 17, 1936, Joe, Mel Ott, and Leiber hit successive triples in the first inning against the Pirates and Eddie Mayo hit one later in the inning. The three in a row and four in an inning are both NL records.

On August 13, 1939, Alex Kampouris, Bill Lohrman, and Joe hit consecutive home runs in the fourth inning. That equalled the existing major league record, accomplished 12 times to that point. The amazing part of this is that it was done by the 8-9-1 batters in the Giants' lineup. Zeke Bonura also homered in the inning, giving New York four, however...

On June 6, 1939, Joe, Harry Danning, Frank Demaree, Burgess Whitehead, and Manny Salvo all homered, also in the fourth inning, to set the still-existing one-inning record with five.

But Joe also established some records on his own:

At the time of his retirement, he was the hardest man to double up in the history of the game. Since records began being kept, he hit into only 48 double plays in 5,053 at bats (1 in 105.3).

In the 1937 World Series, Joe tied the record for a five-game Series with nine hits.

In the 1933 World Series, he had two hits in one inning, also equaling the record.

He was chosen for five All-Star Games.

In ten seasons as the Giants' regular left fielder, he batted over .300 five times (with a high of .331 in 1934) and over .290 twice more. Only in his final season did his career average drop below .300 (to .298).

He had over 200 hits twice and his 205 in 1936 was the last for a Giant for 18 years.

He struck out only once every 22 times at bat for his career.

In 1959, Eddie Brannick, who was then secretary of the club and had been associated with the team since 1906, was asked to name his all-time New York Giants team. Here it is (remember, he saw them all):

Pitchers: Christy Mathewson, Carl Hubbell, Joe McGinnity
Catcher: Roger Bresnahan
First Base: Bill Terry
Second Base: Frankie Frisch
Third Base: Heinie Groh
Shortstop: Travis Jackson
Left Field: Joe Moore
Center Field: Edd Roush
Right Field: Ross Youngs

Today, Joe still lives in the town where he was born, Gause, Texas (he was called the Gause Ghost), in the house he's lived in for over 50 years. And he still loves baseball.

Why were you so difficult to double up?
Joe Moore: I could run. The ground balls, if they bounced enough, you're making time while they're bouncing. These synthetic infields they have now, that ball doesn't bounce much. It's a little faster than it used to be.

We had some good double play combinations in those days when I was playing. We had lots of good shortstops and that's usually the starting of your good double play combinations. Of course, your second baseman has got to handle the ball, too. Most of your double plays are from your shortstop to your second baseman.

I had some real good years for the Giants. I had a decent career. We had a ball club that kinda knew what we were doing and didn't make too many mistakes. I think that's one of the prime things, we didn't make too many mistakes.

You have to have ability—people with ability to do things—and the manager can give all the signs in the world, but if they can't be carried out he's not successful.

You had a .300 career average until your last season.
It was right close there and if things hadn't been like they were, I would have still been with the Giants the next year. I was gonna have to take a little cut and the Indianapolis (American Association) ballclub wanted me. Gabby Hartnett was the manager there and Gabby and I were good friends, so I went there and was actually making more money.

The records today are different from what they were 30, 40, 50 years ago. Used to be, years ago, your shortstop and your second baseman were the only people on the field other than your pitcher that didn't have to hit but about .275. Everybody else had to carry the load. The third baseman and the first baseman and your outfielders were supposed to be your power.

Of course, there were some good shortstops that had good batting averages, too, but you could carry a shortstop and a second baseman, but *everybody* had to hit over .250 then.

Now it's a whole lot different. Now the guys that sit on the bench make more than the stars did in my day. It really is something. When you get right down to it, I think everybody's overpaid. If you do away with television, you're gonna have a depression. Television's paying the way now.

We're living in a different world from what it was 50 years ago. A dollar would buy something 50 years ago. You could buy some land in my country here for five, ten dollars an acre.

You struck out very few times (nine years between 15 and 30 times).

Some guys today strike out 170 times in a season. They've got to be valuable men — they've got to hit some long ones sometime to take care of that.

There was some guy that signed a multi-million dollar contract a year after he hit 11 home runs and drove in 40 runs. I hit in more than 40 runs every year leading off.

I firmly believe this: I don't believe they need the expansion clubs. If anything, they need a reduction. They haven't got good enough ballplayers to fill the bill. We've lowered our standards in a lot of things.

How did the Giants get you?

They bought me from the San Antonio ball club. I was in the Texas League in 1930.

I was just a young boy, 20 or 21 years old, and I had been out in the West Texas League (with Coleman) — Class D, as low as you can get — and it blew up. They couldn't finance it so it disbanded.

My first contract I signed was with San Antonio in 1928 and they sent me out there. It was supposed to have been an option deal, but they didn't have the option papers so they lost me to Coleman. When the ball club blew up, they (San Antonio) re-signed me.

I went to San Antonio and was having a great year in 1930. In fact, I was leading the league. That was when we started playing night ball. I got hit on my throwing (right) arm down around my wrist and broke a bone. I was hitting .380 and they started me back to playing too quick. I wound up with a decent year — I hit .329 even with all that.

When you bat, your wrist goes one way and when you throw, it goes the other way. I could throw pretty good and didn't have much pain, but when I got hold of the bat, that pressure would disturb that thing terribly.

I really didn't fit into the McGraw system because I was small. Another thing about Mr. McGraw, he pretty well had his ball club picked before the season opened. They didn't have farm clubs then and they always bought proven ballplayers. That's one thing that was against me. I was small and coming out of a league that was not as good as the other two Double-A leagues were.

You were the lead-off hitter and you were a notorious first-pitch hitter. The word was not to throw you a strike on the first pitch.

Joe Moore (courtesy of *The National Pastime*).

There was one manager in Cincinnati, if I hit the first ball pitched, it was a $25 fine.

Is it true that Hank Leiber once threatened to beat Dizzy Dean up if he threw at you one more time?

That's right. He told me, "You get out there, 'cause when you get there, I'll be there!" (Laughs) He was big enough to do it, too.

We came pretty near having a riot there that day. That was the nearest thing to a riot I was ever in. It got serious, people got on the field and they didn't have enough cops to stop 'em.

How was Bill Terry as a manager?

There's not many great ballplayers that make good managers. When Terry was a playing manager, I think he was one of the great managers. After they put more responsibility on him — they put him in the office and he was taking care of signing ballplayers and all that stuff — that hurt him a little bit. When he was out there playing with you, our club helped one another. Cooperation was one of our strong points.

Who was the best pitcher?

(Carl) Hubbell was the best pitcher I ever played behind and had the best disposition of any pitcher. He never did get upset if you made mistakes. *Everybody* makes mistakes, but it didn't upset him at all. Some guys, whenever they get upset, it hurts 'em. They can't be themselves after they do that. But it never bothered Hub at all. He'd just coast all through it.

Who was the toughest pitcher on you?

One of the toughest pitchers on me was a fellow over at Pittsburgh, a boy named Cy Blanton.

His son lives here in Texas now about a hundred miles from where I live and he stopped by here and visited with me a year or so ago. He's a real nice young man and he told me it was a sad story with his father. He said his father drank himself to death. That's hurt a lot of 'em. He was young (when he died) — 35 or so.

Pittsburgh had lots of that. You know, Paul Waner didn't take real good care of himself. I don't know *what* he would have done if he'd taken care of himself. He could do everything that anybody else could do with a bat. He's the best hitter I ever saw. His lifetime average was up there at .330-something, which is a good average and there's some higher than that, but I don't believe there's anybody could handle the bat any better than he could.

The little one (Lloyd Waner) — we were talking about that ball hitting the ground — if that ball hit the ground twice when Little Waner was young, he was already past first base. (Laughs)

They were different. Both of 'em were quiet, they didn't have much to say. They weren't snooty or anything like that, they just didn't talk much.

Little Waner didn't hardly talk at all. There were a few people he talked to. Hughie Critz was one fellow that could get lots of conversation out of Little Waner. They were both small men and they had a bet on about hitting home runs for the year. I think one is about all that either one of 'em ever hit. (Laughs)

Is there one game that stands out?

I think one of the greatest games in my playing days was when we played the Cardinals all day. Hubbell pitched an 18-inning ballgame and beat 'em one-to-nothing (Tex Carleton pitched 16 innings for St. Louis), and then we turned around in the second game and (Roy) Parmalee beat Diz, one-to-nothing. We played 27 innings and made two runs and won two ballgames. (Laughs) (It happened on July 2, 1933.)

Did you save any souvenirs from your playing days?

I have two grandchildren and I've given them nearly everything.

I still have a few things. I have the ball that President (Franklin) Roosevelt signed that he threw out in the 1937 All-Star Game. He autographed it for me.

Do you get much fan mail today?

I certainly do. I get some *good* fan mail, too, on the average of ten letters a week.

I want to brag on myself a little bit. I came out of baseball and I don't think I have any enemies in baseball. I played to win, but I never played to hurt anybody. I was popular in New York. Even in Brooklyn I was popular. For a Giant to be popular in Brooklyn, that's outstanding. (Laughs) They always treated me fair over there, there was never any of those fruits and vegetables thrown out when I went out the field.

Sometimes people cause people to be that way toward 'em by the things they do and the things they say. Lots of times it pays to keep your mouth shut. (Laughs)

Our ballclub was popular on the road. We were really more popular than the Yankees were in the road. The Yankees didn't play to near as many people in St. Louis as we did. We always had a full house in Chicago, too.

We were a good ballclub to watch. If they wanted to see a good ballgame, that's where they came.

Would you be a ballplayer again?

That was my life's ambition — to be a ballplayer — from a baby on up. I have a picture when I was a little bitty boy and I had a ball in my hand then. Everybody said I was born with a ball in my hand. (Laughs)

A few years ago I was elected to the Texas Hall of Fame. Another boy from the Giants, Homer Peel, is from around here and he's in there, too.

Any regrets?

Not a great deal. I'm pretty well satisfied. Of course, I'd have liked to have been better. I always liked to improve. I gave it all I had and it was good to me. We didn't get rich like they are now, but we had a whole lot more fun, I think.

Our ballclub was a family ballclub. All the boys that had families lived up in the same neighborhood in New York and we'd get together at night and had Ping-Pong tables and all that kind of stuff. We were just family, that's all.

Now they tell me, whenever that last man's out they get to the showers and get out of there and they don't see each other until the next day.

We'd sit around at night — like at that hotel there in Pittsburgh that had that big porch out front — and replay the ballgame. They don't do that anymore.

* * *

Here are the ten hardest and ten easiest men to double up (minimum 5,000 at bats since GIDP records were first kept — 1933 NL, 1939 AL).

Hardest	AB	DP	AB/DP	Easiest	AB	DP	AB/DP
*Brett Butler	6169	47	131.3	Ernie Lombardi	5260	261	20.1
Mickey Rivers	5629	44	127.9	George Scott	7433	287	25.9
Don Blasingame	5296	43	123.2	Jim Rice	8225	311	26.4
JOE MOORE	5053	48	105.3	Rico Carty	5606	206	27.2
Richie Ashburn	8365	83	100.8	Joe Torre	7874	184	27.7
Cesar Tovar	5569	58	96.0	*Julio Franco	5416	194	27.9
Stan Hack	7100	78	91.0	Lou Piniella	5867	209	28.1
Bill Nicholson	5534	61	90.7	Jackie Jensen	5236	185	28.30
Lou Brock	10332	114	90.6	*Tony Pena	5550	196	28.32
Wally Moses	5188	58	89.4	Bill Jurges	5564	195	28.5

*Through 1992

JOSEPH GREGG (JO-JO, THE GAUSE GHOST) MOORE
Born December 25, 1908, Gause, TX
Ht. 5'11" Wt. 155 Batted Left Threw Right

Year	Team	G	AB	R	H	2B	3B	HR	RBI	SB	BA	SA
1930	NYN	3	5	1	1	0	0	0	0	0	.200	.200
1931		4	8	0	2	1	0	0	3	1	.250	.375
1932		86	361	53	110	15	2	2	27	4	.305	.374
1933		132	524	56	153	16	5	0	42	4	.292	.342
1934		139	580	106	192	37	4	15	61	5	.331	.486
1935		155	681*	108	201	28	9	15	71	5	.295	.429
1936		152	649	110	205	29	9	7	63	2	.316	.421
1937		142	580	89	180	37	10	6	57	7	.310	.440
1938		125	506	76	153	23	6	11	56	2	.302	.437

Year	Team	G	AB	R	H	2B	3B	HR	RBI	SB	BA	SA
1939	NYN	138	562	80	151	23	2	10	47	5	.269	.370
1940		138	543	83	150	33	4	6	46	7	.276	.385
1941		121	428	47	117	16	2	7	40	4	.273	.369
12 years		1335	5427	809	1615	258	53	79	513	46	.298	.408

*Led league

World Series

Year	Team	G	AB	R	H	2B	3B	HR	RBI	SB	BA	SA
1933	NYN	5	22	1	5	1	0	0	1	0	.227	.273
1936		6	28	4	6	2	0	1	1	0	.214	.393
1937		5	23	1	9	1	0	0	1	0	.391	.435
3 years		16	73	6	20	4	0	1	3	0	.273	.370

All-Star Game

Year	League	G	AB	R	H	2B	3B	HR	RBI	SB	BA	SA
1935	National	1	2	0	0	0	0	0	0	0	.000	.000
1936			Selected, did not play									
1937		1	1	0	0	0	0	0	0	0	.000	.000
1938			Selected, did not play									
1940		1	2	0	0	0	0	0	0	0	.000	.000
5 years		3	5	0	0	0	0	0	0	0	.000	.000

PAT MULLIN

Pat Mullin (courtesy of Detroit Tigers).

Four Years to the War
AL All-Star 1947, 1948

"I always had pretty good luck against left-handed pitchers until they got the idea that a left-handed hitter wasn't supposed to hit against lefthanders..."

— Pat Mullin

Pat Mullin today is considered, by those who remember him, to have been a journeyman ballplayer.

Maybe he was, but how different it may have been had World War II not taken four years of his prime. He was the top rookie in the American League in 1941 when sidelined by a mid-season injury and the next season the military laid claim to him. But he showed what he could do in 1949 when allowed to play a full season: .288, 11 triples, 23 home runs, 91 runs, 80 RBI's, 77 walks vs. 57 strikeouts, .504 slugging pct.

That year, 1949, he *started* in right field for the American League in the All-Star Game. He had also been selected in 1948, when a late-season illness cost him what had begun as a top year.

Pat was a hustler in the true sense of the word and he knew (and still knows) the game. He contributed to it long after his playing days ended. He should be remembered for more than being a journeyman.

Were you originally signed by the Tigers?
Pat Mullin: Yes, in August 1936.
But you didn't play until the next year.
I finished my last year of high school and graduated in 1937. I was still in high school when they signed me.
You began '37 at Beaumont (Texas League) and were doing pretty well but they sent you to Lake Charles (Evangeline League), where evidently you overmatched most of the fellows in the league (.383, 29 doubles, 17 triples, 16 home runs, 89 RBI's, 109 runs, .656 slg. pct.).
When I went to spring training with Beaumont, there were 90 minor league players there. An awful lot of those players had played three or four years of minor league ball already.

I was signed as a catcher and when I went down there I worked out as a catcher, but I had better speed than what they, or I, realized — with the catcher's stuff on I would beat some of the batters to first base on a ground ball to the infield. So they asked me if I ever played the outfield, which I had, and they put me in the outfield.

Our manager, Al Vincent, had been operated on and wasn't on the roster when the season started, so out of the 90 guys I was the only rookie to stay (with Beaumont). I got in a few games, pinch-hit some, and I think I wound up hitting three–something. When the manager got over his operation and was able to play, somebody had to go. I was the only rookie there so it was me.

Our minor league ballclub — that is, Detroit's — was Alexandria, Louisiana, and all my friends that were there in spring training had already been shipped out to Alexandria. In order to place me, they sent me to Lake Charles, Louisiana, on option, so that's where I played my first year.

Did you ever catch professionally?
No, I never caught a game of pro ball.
In '38 you rejoined Beaumont and played there again in '39 and went to Buffalo (International League) in '40. You were amazingly consistent those three years (.275, .278, .273; 67, 61, and 61 RBI's). You first joined the Tigers in 1940.
I came up the last two weeks of 1940.
Where did you start in '41, Buffalo or Detroit?
In spring training in 1941, I was hopeful of going north with the ballclub and being with Detroit. The general manager at that time was Jack Zeller. He called me outside the hotel in spring training and he said, "Pat, the manager," which was Del Baker, "thinks that you ought to go north with the club. I think that you ought to go back to Buffalo and play until Hank Greenberg goes into the Army." See, Hank was due to go in. "What do you think?"
I said, "Well, I agree with you." I would rather be at Buffalo playing than to sit on the bench in the major leagues and when the time would come that I would get the chance to come up with Detroit I would have been playing and be in pretty good groove.
When you got the chance you did great.
(Laughs) I was hitting better in the major leagues than I did in the minors.
Were you able to finish out '41 or did the service take you before the season ended?
On July 2, I think, we were playing a night game in Chicago against the White Sox and I hit a ball to the right of Joe Kuhel, the first baseman. It looked like a base hit and I'm going down the line and the pitcher, (Bill) Dietrich, came running over to cover first base and, somehow, in an awkward way, he was on his stomach with his feet on the bag — both feet. As I got to the bag I tried to step in between his feet and legs, not to tramp on him, and my foot got caught under one of his legs and I guess I went straight up in the air like I was coming off a diving board and hit on my right shoulder and dislocated my shoulder and was out the rest of the year. And I was doing so well, all my dreams were coming true.
Then Uncle Sam called.
That's right, in '42.
You lost four years when you'd have been right at your peak.
Yeah.
Did you get to play ball in the service?
Yes, I did. I never got overseas. I went to a reception center at New Cumberland, Pennsylvania. I was down at the siding getting ready to get on the train and my name was called out and I was sent back to my barracks and was told that the colonel wanted a baseball team. So I was at New Cumberland, oh, a couple of years and we had a baseball club. We had fellows like Tommy Hughes, who pitched for the Phillies, and Elmer Valo and guys like

that. As they came into the reception center I would go to the Special Services captain and tell him, "I'd like to have this guy," so we had a pretty good ballclub.

From there, when they started to ship everybody out, they shipped me to Special Services headquarters in Alabama. A lot of the guys I had at New Cumberland followed and we won the championship of Alabama and played Johnny Pesky's Naval team in Atlanta and went all around. We played teams like the Camp Campbell Armored Division and did very well.

Before I was shipped out of New Cumberland, I was named on Mickey Cochrane's All-Service team, which trained at Great Lakes Naval Station.

When you returned from the service, you weren't as sharp as when you went in.

I couldn't throw as well as before I hurt my shoulder, but knowing how to play the hitters and how to charge the ball and get rid of it kept me in the major leagues.

When I came back in '46 I didn't do that well. In '47 I started off *real* good and was named to the All-Star team but toward the end of the season I came up with the flu or something — I don't know what I had — and I wouldn't tell anybody. I kept playing and I'd be out there and a cold sweat would come over me but I didn't want anybody to think I was trying to get out of the lineup. In fact, one day I was going to tell Steve O'Neill (the manager) that I didn't feel right but I didn't do it. First time up I hit a home run and I was ashamed to go tell him I didn't feel good. (Laughs)

All throughout my career, because I couldn't throw as well as the other guys, I filled in and pinch-hit and got quite a number of games in. I was thrilled to death to think I was still in the major leagues.

In 1948 you had a super season. Today someone would be paid $2 million for that kind of production.

Oh, yeah.

Nineteen fifty-three was your last year in the majors and you came back in '63 as a coach. What happened in the ten years in between?

In '54 I went with Billy Hitchcock to Buffalo. He was the manager and I was a playing coach. Sometime in May or June that year, the manager at Little Rock, Bill Norman, quit, so I was sent down there as the playing manager for the rest of the year.

In 1955 I was the playing manager at Idaho Falls, Idaho, all in the Detroit organization. In '56 I was at Jamestown, New York, as the playing manager. I was operated on during the season and, of course, I was out the rest of the year.

In '57 I went to Detroit as a scout working under Ed Katalinas — he signed Al Kaline and fellows like that. I scouted for Detroit from '57 on to '63 when I was hired as a coach under Charlie Dressen.

Pat Mullin (courtesy of *The National Pastime*).

As a scout, did you sign anybody we'd know?

One of the guys that did very well was Gates Brown. I signed him out of prison. He kept his nose clean and did a fine job.

I had a guy, (Doug) Gallagher, that got to the big leagues — a left-handed pitcher. He hurt his arm but he had a good fastball and a good curveball. I signed Chip Lang for Montreal, a right-handed pitcher that got a cup of coffee but things didn't work out for him. And Ray Oyler, the shortstop.

In one of my first assignments to scout organized ball I went out to Iowa and recommended, if he was ever available, Denny McLain. He was playing Class D ball. The next spring, along with Denny, Chicago (White Sox) had another pitcher and they couldn't protect both of 'em so they tried to sneak Denny through and not protect him. Detroit drafted him and you know the story from there on — he turned out to be a 30-game winner.

Katalinas, Stubby Overmire, and I went over to Sarasota to the Chicago White Sox minor league spring training. We drove over there in a station wagon to pick up Denny and went upstairs and they were having an organization meeting. The way they looked at us, they kind of snickered that we were going to get Denny. I guess that they'd had their problems with him. We took Denny back to Lakeland and he went out and did a good job in our minor league setup.

After I left, I guess when Mayo Smith came in as the manager, I read a lot of things about Denny — not paying rent for his airplane parking and all that stuff.

Seeing him in Class D, he had a good fastball, not a real good curve, a change-up, a sort of sharp slider. I felt kind of close to him. I was sorry to see him get into all the doggone trouble he got into because he had the world by the tail.

Another guy that I scouted was Steve Boros at the University of Michigan. When they had Steve in while he was still in school, I guess he told John McHale and Ed Katalinas that when he signed he wanted me to sign him. That made me feel real good.

How was Charlie Dressen to work under?

When I first went there, a lot of guys said, "Boy, Pat, he's tough!" But he was really wonderful to all the coaches — Bob Swift, Stubby Overmire, and myself. We all came there at one time — we joined the ballclub in Boston and so did Charlie. That was when they let Bob Scheffing go.

Being in the minor league setup as a scout and as an instructor in spring training, I got to know Bob. I went up to him and said, "Bob, I always thought that if I was going to be a major league coach I would rather come as your coach rather than come in the day that you were let go." Bob said, "Pat, I asked for you two or three times." I guess they thought I was doing pretty good as a scout.

In 1966, the Tigers got off to a terrific start and then Dressen died. Bob Swift took over and he died. Frank Skaff finished the season as the manager. The team did not do as well in the second half—having two managers die in one season I guess is unprecedented. How did it affect the players?

Nobody really came out and said how they felt, but, whether you realize it or not, there's something in there that isn't the same. That was a big blow, losing Charlie and Bob.

Charlie was really, I thought, fair and wonderful to the players. He wasn't hard to get along with. As far as the coaches were concerned, anybody that did things for Charlie, he'd say, "How about my coaches?" So we were in everything that he was in.

In Montreal, you coached under a very successful manager, Dick Williams. What do you think of him?

I said to Dick, "You know, Dick, with *all* the things that go on in modern baseball I really give you credit for how you handle things." Some guy might pop off and say things to the players, but Dick had been through the mill and he handled everything very well.

I was up there (Montreal) as a minor league and major league hitting coach then. If we had a guy in the minor leagues they might send me down there for five days or so. They sent me to Denver to work with (Tim) Wallach and to Memphis to work with Terry Francona when they signed him. Both guys really made me look good because after I left they were hitting the ball real well. Guys would say when I came back to Montreal, "What in the world are you telling those guys down there?!" I said, "The same things I tell you but they listened."

Francona looked like he was going to set the world on fire.

They thought when they signed him and sent him there they would try to get him to pull the ball and hit for some power — hit some home runs — but Terry wasn't that kind of a hitter. He was a guy that would slap that ball to all fields, had good bat control, and made contact. My recommendation was I'd rather have a guy hit .340 with ten home runs than a guy hit .220 with 25 or 30.

Tell us about Gary Carter.

I had him his first year. He came to Jamestown where we had our rookie spring training and from there they went to Cocoa Beach. Two or three times during the year I would go there and sometimes maybe be there for ten days.

I had Carter right out of high school. He was like he plays ball in the major leagues, just a bundle of energy, full of life, hustled, bore down. The thing about Gary, and I used to sit and talk with him, was he had power to all fields but Gary wanted to pull that ball. Like in batting practice, if he didn't hit five or ten out he thought it was a bad batting practice. I used to try to get him to understand that if he, as a catcher, had a guy up there hitting who was trying to pull everything, he would have his pitcher pitch him down low and away. Usually when you try to overpower the pitcher's pitch you hit a ground ball down to short, over to first, go get a drink.

To me, I thought that he had a great arm, he handled the pitchers well, he received well, hustled — my God, he really hustled — didn't have great speed, had the power. The thing we were trying to do was to have him not be a one-way type of a hitter, not always pull that ball.

When they pitched him down low and away, if Gary tried to pull that ball he would look terrible on some of them. On that same pitch, if he'd go with it, he could put the ball out in right-center.

In your playing days, who were the best hitters you saw?

Ted Williams, Joe DiMaggio. Playing against those guys, I thought, "Boy-oh-boy, they could really hit that ball!"

Guys like Hank Greenberg, Charlie Gehringer on the Detroit ballclub — they ended up in the Hall of Fame.

Who was the best all-around ballplayer?

I would say Joe DiMaggio — fielding, throwing, hitting, he had power, he was a good base runner. I would take Ted Williams as my hitter.

I didn't see Stan Musial that much, he was in the National League. Stan only lived about ten miles from where I lived — he lived in Donora, Pennsylvania.

Who were the best pitchers?

When I first came up, Washington had a lot of those knuckleballers. Of course, I hit against guys like Bob Feller, Bobby Shantz, Bob Lemon — he was always tough, he'd start that ball outside and you'd swear to God it was going to be a ball and at the last second it would just hit that outside corner.

I didn't play against (Hal) Newhouser and (Dizzy) Trout and (Virgil) Trucks, but they were great pitchers.

Who was the toughest pitcher on you?

A guy that could change speeds real well, that didn't throw as hard as Feller, would give me more trouble than Feller. I think a guy like Bob Lemon, who could hit those corners real well, was real tough on me.

You were a left-handed batter. I expected you to name a southpaw.

Well, you know, I always had pretty good luck against left-handed pitchers until they got the idea that a left-handed hitter wasn't supposed to hit against left-handers, started to two-platoon. Of course, I didn't get to play against 'em very much then, but up until they started to do that two-platooning I felt that I was holding my own and doing all right against them.

What was your best game?

In 1949 we went into Yankee Stadium, Red Rolfe was the manager and I hadn't started a game, I think, for 40 games. I was just pinch-hitting and stuff. We were going to play the Yankees a double-header. I walked into the clubhouse — it was on a Sunday — and somebody said, "Pat, Red wants to see you." Whenever you haven't been playing, you think, "I wonder if I'm traded or they've let me go or what?"

When I went in he said, "Whatever game they pitch a right-hander I'm going to give John Groth a rest." It was the second game of the double-header — Vic Raschi started. I hit a home run the first time up, I got an infield hit the next time, then I think I walked, then I hit another home run, then I walked again, then I hit *another* home run! It turned out to be a slugfest, I think the score was 12–8 or something like that. I went to bat six times: I was walked twice, hit three home runs and a single, and I was the next hitter, with one man out and a man on first base and Johnny Lipon hit into a double play. Of course, I may have struck out the next time up, but that one more chance, the way things were going for me, would have been nice. I was the most surprised guy in the park over it.

That's when we still left the gloves on the field. I went out to get my glove and couldn't find it. Here the umpire had it under his arm, hiding it from me. When I went over to get it, the umpire said, "Keep going, Pat, keep going." They were pulling for me.

What do you think of the changes in the game in the last 50 years?

You hear a lot of people talk about all the money that the players are making. I have to be honest, sometimes I can't believe what the heck they're making, but I feel more power to 'em.

When I first came up I was making $4,500 and was thrilled to death to be in the big leagues. I couldn't believe I was going to walk on a major league diamond. I guess back then, a guy like Enos Slaughter, an established player, was making about twelve-five.

In the 1940 World Series — Detroit lost to Cincinnati — losing share was about 4,000-something. Today I think it's about 90 — way up there.

When I went back up as a coach, not only with Detroit but with Montreal, the way they travel, they never see their luggage. It used to be whatever we rode the trains and we'd get into St. Louis the train might be a half a mile from the station and we carried our suitcase into the station and got into a cab and went. Like now, when a ballgame is over and they're going to go on the road, their things are packed, they never touch their luggage, they go to the plane, they give them that big meal money, then they come around and want to know if you want steak or lobster, this or that, and the ballclub's paying for that and they've got the meal money in their pockets.

When I was first coming up with Detroit, and I guess other ballclubs did it, they didn't give you the cash. You signed a ticket at the hotel you stayed in. I think it's much better if they give you the cash. If you don't want to eat at the hotel you can go wherever you want to go — Italian, seafood, or whatever.

They make more in meal money than we made in a season.

Did you save souvenirs from your career?

I have the first glove that I ever used in the big leagues — it looks like a little handglove. I have a uniform from Montreal. I have a Detroit uniform.

I didn't save a whole lot, but my wife has a scrapbook that she put things in.

Do you have any of your baseball cards?

I don't have all of them, but I have a couple of them. I have the '52 reprint, it's in good shape. When they did the reprint they sent me the whole set.

I get letters maybe three or four times a week and sometimes there's a baseball card in there and I think to myself, "Now, where in the world did they get this one?"

Do you honor autograph requests?

Yes. I sign it as soon as I get it — cards or index cards — and they usually have a self-addressed envelope and I have it ready to go out in the mail the next morning. If anyone takes the time to send it I'm going to get it back out in the mail and get it back to 'em.

If you went back over 50 years, would you do it again?

Yeah, and I'll tell you why. As a young boy back here in the coal mines, my dream and my ambition was to someday be a major league ballplayer. I'd get up in the morning, especially in the summertime, I'd have my cereal or whatever it was, my mother would put my dad out to work — he worked in a coal mine — I had my bat, which was tacked, a roll of tape to tape the ball when we needed it, and I took off for the ball diamond.

We played all day. If we didn't have enough for two teams then we'd play scrub or we'd wind up playing Indian ball. And I was gone all day — looked forward to it every day and felt terrible the days it rained.

All my prayers were answered.

As an active player and as a coach with Detroit and with Cleveland with Joe Adcock and with Montreal I'm just short of 18 years, major league–wise. The time I spent with Montreal as a coach, I was already drawing my pension so it didn't count, pension-wise. I enjoyed it all.

Did you leave baseball when you left Montreal?

No, I went back as the minor league hitting coach. I finally called it quits in '85.

PATRICK JOSEPH MULLIN
Born November 1, 1917, Trotter, PA
Ht. 6'2"   Wt. 190   Batted Left Threw Right

Year	Team	G	AB	R	H	2B	3B	HR	RBI	SB	BA	SA
1940	DetA	4	4	0	0	0	0	0	0	0	.000	.000
1941		54	220	42	76	11	5	5	23	5	.345	.509
1946		93	276	34	68	13	4	3	35	3	.246	.355
1947		116	398	62	102	28	6	15	62	3	.256	.470
1948		138	496	91	143	16	11	23	80	1	.288	.504

Year	Team	G	AB	R	H	2B	3B	HR	RBI	SB	BA	SA
1949	DetA	104	310	55	83	8	6	12	59	1	.268	.448
1950		69	142	16	31	5	0	6	23	1	.218	.380
1951		110	295	41	83	11	6	12	51	2	.281	.481
1952		97	255	29	64	13	5	7	35	4	.251	.424
1953		79	97	11	26	1	0	4	17	0	.268	.402
10 years		864	2493	381	676	106	43	87	385	20	.271	.453

All-Star Game

Year	League	G	AB	R	H	2B	3B	HR	RBI	SB	BA	SA
1947	American			Selected, did not play								
1948		1	1	0	0	0	0	0	0	1	.000	.000

ANDY PAFKO

Andy Pafko (courtesy of *The National Pastime*).

Handy Andy
NL All-Star 1947, 1948, 1949, 1950

"I never caused any trouble, I kept my nose clean, I hustled all the time, I gave it an all-out effort..."
— Andy Pafko

Several players over the decades have been very popular with the fans, but, except in the cases of superstars destined for the Hall of Fame, that popularity gradually wanes once the glove is hung up for good. A very few, though, attain a level of popularity that endures — it does not abate as the years pass. One of these is Andy Pafko.

Andy was an excellent ballplayer, although superstar status escaped him. Nonetheless, he hit 213 home runs and compiled a .285 average in 17 big league seasons. He batted over .300 three times and had seasons of 26, 30, and 36 homers, averaging 20 a year from 1948 through 1954.

From time to time there appears in various periodicals a list of batters who hit a lot of home runs and struck out fewer times. Joltin' Joe is always there, and Big Klu and Stan the Man and the Splendid Splinter and a few others, but Andy Pafko is often not included.

Well, include him. In 1950, Andy hit 36 home runs, second in the NL only to Ralph Kiner's 47, and whiffed only 32 times! He batted .304 and drove in 92 runs for a Cubs team that finished a soundly-beaten seventh, scoring the fewest runs in the league and having the lowest batting average (by a full ten points!). The table at the end of this chapter lists all players who hit 35 or more home runs in a season and struck out fewer than 35 times.

This was not a fluke season for Andy. In eight of the ten seasons he went to the plate enough times to qualify for the batting title, he struck out fewer than 40 times (only 23 in 469 at bats as a rookie in 1944). In four All-Star Games, he went 4-for-10. Okay, maybe he wasn't a superstar, but he *was* a great player.

Everywhere you played — Chicago, Brooklyn, Milwaukee — you were one of the most popular players on the team. Why?

Andy Pafko: Well, I never caused any trouble, I kept my nose clean, I hustled all the time, I gave it an all-out effort — dove for the ball, slid into bases, and all that. I guess the fans realized I always gave it my best effort.

You came up late in 1943 after a big year at Los Angeles (Pacific Coast League). How did you avoid the service?

I always had trouble with high blood pressure. I never realized it until I took my draft physical. I've been on medication for many years since then. I have to watch my weight and what I eat and it's under control. It never affected my playing.

You stepped into the starting lineup as a rookie in '44 and then in '45 you had a great year.

Yes, I think I hit not quite .300, maybe .298, and drove in some hundred runs (110). I think I was runner-up to Phil Cavarretta as Most Valuable Player in 1945. That was as close as I ever came. He had a great year, hit nearly .360 or so, led the league.

In '46 you were hurt and missed a lot of time. What happened?

Was that '46? I ran into the center field wall catching a line drive and broke my arm.

In '48 you played third base all season. How did that come about?

That was quite an experience. I had never played third base. I had played for Milt Stock — he was Eddie Stanky's father-in-law — down in Macon, Georgia, and he knew I had a good arm and was a good fielder. When spring training opened in '48 the Cubs had no third baseman. Stan Hack had retired after 1947. They tried me at third and I worked out and was the starting third baseman when the season opened.

The previous year I had made the All-Star team as a center fielder and then in '48 I made it as the starting third baseman. In '49 I went back to the outfield and made the All-Star team again and then again in 1950.

In 1950 you became one of only a handful of players in history to hit over 30 home runs and have fewer strikeouts than homers.

There was a small article in the *Chicago Sun-Times* about that, Eddie Gold wrote it. I didn't realize it until then.

Over the years you never struck out often.

I never considered myself a home run hitter. I was more of a contact hitter. I tried to meet the ball. I was never much of a pull hitter, I was a gap hitter. I never tried to hit a home run, but I got my share over the years.

Did you enjoy your years in Chicago?

Oh, yes. That was my first team, I came through their minor league system. I was delighted to be a Cub.

Then I was traded away in 1951, which was a big disappointment at the time. There were no rumors or anything, so it was a shock.

I went from a team going downhill to a real good team, so I should have been happy but Chicago was home, I established myself here, I met my wife in Chicago.

Eventually, though, it was the best thing that ever happened to me. I went to a real good ballclub with great talent. That was the year we got beat in the play-off by Bobby Thomson's home run. But then in '52 we won and played in the World Series. That was a big thrill, my second World Series.

You were in a bunch of World Series.

Yes, the Cubs on '45 and after I left the Dodgers I went over to Milwaukee and played in two more. In '57 we were World Champions. That was a big thrill for me. I was born and raised in Wisconsin and that was more or less like coming home.

You were traded to the Boston Braves, weren't you?

Yes, in the spring of '53 I joined the Boston Braves in spring training and then we made the switch in spring training. When the season opened we moved right into Milwaukee.

The Braves had been a very bad team in '52.

Right, way down in the standings. I think they only made two trades over the winter. They acquired me from the Dodgers and they also got Joe Adcock from the Cincinnati Reds. And we gave a good account that year and as the years went by we got better and better and finally won the pennant in '57.

We had some great, great talent. We had Warren Spahn and Lew Burdette and Buhl and Mathews and Aaron and Schoendienst and Crandall. We had a heck of a ballclub.

Back to Brooklyn — did you like it there?

I liked it. We had a real good ballclub, a lot of talent. I still consider that one of the greatest clubs ever assembled. We had Hodges, Robinson, Reese, Cox, Campanella — Furillo, Snider, and me in the outfield. We had a great pitching staff: Carl Erskine, Joe Black, Preacher Roe. Ebbets Field was a great ballpark.

The trade that brought me over was an eight-player trade, four-for-four. The Cubs got Gene Hermanski, Joe Hatten, Eddie Miksis, and Bruce Edwards. Along with me were Wayne Terwilliger, Johnny Schmitz, and Rube Walker. A pitcher, a catcher, an infielder, and an outfielder went each way. I think there was some money involved, but I never knew how much.

At first it shook me up but after a couple of days I settled down. It was a break for me financially and I went to a real good club.

It was June 15, the trading deadline. I remember it like it was just yesterday. Brooklyn was in Chicago for a three-game series. We were standing around the batting cage at the second game of the series. The Dodgers came on the field and big Don Newcombe yelled at me, "Hey, Pafko, you're going to be a Dodger tomorrow!" There must have been something in the New York papers because there had been nothing in the Chicago papers.

When that game was over I went home and sat down to dinner and, lo and behold, the phone rang and it was the Cubs' front office. They said they'd just made a big trade and I was involved. My wife cried.

The next day I moved my stuff from one side of the field to the Dodgers' side and played against my old team that day.

That was difficult. Quite a shock.

Was the trade to the Braves as tough as the one to Brooklyn?

Well, once you've been traded it's easier to take the second time. I was a little disappointed. I was going from a good club to a real bad club — Boston. But in spring training we became Milwaukee and that helped. I was going back home and the club turned out to be great.

We won the pennant in '57 and '58 and should have won four straight years. We just lost in '56 and then lost a play-off in '59, when the Dodgers beat us out.

Andy Pafko (courtesy of *The National Pastime*).

But I have no complaints. I played in four World Series. I played on three different clubs and all three won pennants.

Jack Brickhouse, the announcer here in Chicago, told me I was the only one who played on three clubs in the *same* league and *all* three made it to the World Series. And it was only an eight-team league then.

Who were the best players you saw?

I think the *best* player was Stan "the Man" Musial. He was the epitome of the great ballplayer — he could do it all. And he was a gentleman on and off the field.

There were others — Willie Mays, Duke Snider, Jackie Robinson — but I think Stan the Man was by far the greatest.

What about pitchers?

The toughest for me, with no hesitation, was Ewell Blackwell of Cincinnati. He was the toughest I ever faced. Thank goodness I only saw him two or three times a year.

There were a lot of other guys who would give me a tough time, like Sal "the Barber" Maglie and Robin Roberts, but Blackwell was the toughest on me, without a doubt.

You played 17 years. What was your top salary?

My top salary was $35,000.

What do you think of today's salaries?

(Laughs) When the old-timers get together at old-timers' games, that's the first thing we discuss — the salaries of the modern-day players. I don't begrudge them anything, more power to them.

But I think we played in a better era. There were 16 ballclubs. Now there's 26. I think the quality's diluted. There's not enough talent to go around.

One of the troubles with modern-day ballplayers is they go for home runs. They don't play sound ball. And each club has players who still belong in the minors.

Kids don't spend enough time developing. Years ago, players spent four, five, six years in the minors; now they rush them in a year or two. They don't learn the fundamentals. I managed in the farm system for six or seven years for the Braves. These kids come out of high school or college and make simple mistakes, things they should have been taught. They're rushed too fast.

We had to earn our jobs. Kids today don't have to work hard, it's all handed to them.

What are the major changes you've seen in baseball?

First of all, the money. And then, of course, artificial turf and indoor stadiums. Jet travel from coast to coast. Night games — many more than we played. I never thought I'd live to see lights in Wrigley Field.

Any changes you think should be made?

Well, money again. The public doesn't like it. It costs a family of four $75 to $100 to go to a game now — tickets, food, parking, and all. This is one way those big salaries are paid and it's tough on the average working man.

What was the attitude toward autographs in your day?

Today, a lot of parks have ways for the players to avoid the fans. Years ago, we'd sit in the bus and we'd open the windows and kids would surround the bus and we'd sign autographs through the open windows until the bus left.

Today I hear some of the players won't give you the time of day.

One way or the other, the fans pay the salaries. The ballplayers should remember that.

And a ballplayer should be a role model. Now all you hear about is drugs, big money, and so on. Guaranteed contracts were never dreamed of in my day. You got paid year by year on how you performed. You didn't get paid for the next five years on what you did last year. I don't mind a guy getting paid money if he performs. If he knocks in so many runs or wins so many games, pay him; but don't pay him if he doesn't perform.

The incentive is gone, the desire. A guy gets a hangnail today, he can't play. Pay should be one year at a time.

So you think a ballplayer should be a role model?

They should, definitely!

Like Sparky Anderson. He likes all his ballplayers to be clean-cut, clean shaven. No long hair. That's a disgrace! And the chains! I've never seen so many guys with gold chains! I guess that's the money difference. And the attitude is different.

The fans, the kids, look up to them. Sometimes the kids worship a ballplayer more than their mom and dad. I'm not saying that's right, but it happens. The ballplayers should set an example.

I had a role model when I was growing up — my guy was Joe DiMaggio. I'll never forget, I played my first All-Star Game in Chicago in 1947. I was the center fielder for the National League and Joe DiMaggio was the center fielder for the American. What a thrill — for me to be in the same ballpark with my hero, in center field! I came up to the plate and I got a base hit over second base. Who fielded my base hit? Joe DiMaggio!

Today when I run into DiMaggio at a card show somewhere I always bring that up to him. Even today, I look up to him. And he's never disappointed me. What a great ballplayer and person! I even get goosebumps talking to you about him now.

And I feel this way as a ballplayer. How do you think some of these kids feel seeing their heroes and being ignored? It's awfully disappointing.

I've never heard anyone say anything bad about you.

Thank you. I've tried to keep my nose clean and stay out of trouble. It's the easiest thing in the world to do. I never drank, I went to bed on time, I reported to the ballpark on time. No one could say anything bad. That's part of being a role model.

Did you save souvenirs from your career?

I was never a real collector.

I've got some autographed baseballs. One is autographed by Ty Cobb when he came to Milwaukee to visit Fred Haney. They were teammates on the Detroit Tigers. I've got one signed by Nixon when he was the vice president. I've got Joe DiMaggio's autograph.

I was in Washington, D.C., when Ronald Reagan was still president. The Emil Verban Society invited some of the Cubs' players. We were supposed to meet the president, but he had to have a press conference over the Libyan trouble and we missed meeting him. But I left a ball with one of his aides and Ronald Reagan signed it. I treasure it. He signed it, "To Andy Pafko, from one fan to another. Ronald Reagan." That's on my mantel in the family room.

Do you receive much fan mail?

I get more now than when I played. I get fan mail from second and third generation kids from all over the country. I get five or six or sometimes even ten fan letters a day from all over. Alaska. Canada. It's amazing.

Do you answer?

Every one. I'm retired now, I have little else to do. I read them all and answer. Definitely. If a kid takes time to send you a letter and ask for your autograph, you have to answer.

I don't know why a lot of these guys today, making all that money, don't answer. It's wrong. It's beyond me. I can't figure it out. It takes a little time, that's all.

Is there one game that stands out in your memory?

There's no hesitation. I played in four World Series and four All-Star Games, but the one biggest thrill ever was in 1945.

My mother and dad never saw me play a big league ballgame. They came down to Chicago from Wisconsin. We were playing Pittsburgh. The bases were loaded and I came up and struck out on a three-and-two count. This was the first game of a double-header. My mother was sitting in the stands hoping I would do something worthwhile.

Well, two or three innings later the same situation came up. The bases were loaded, there were two out, and I hit a grand slam off of Preacher Roe, who later became my teammate with the Dodgers. I'll never forget it.

Everyone was cheering. My mom was sitting there with my dad behind the dugout. They didn't know anything about baseball, they came over from Europe.

Finally someone explained to them that that was the best thing a player could do — hit a home run with the bases loaded. She finally got up and started clapping. When I saw that I had tears in my eyes. I'll never forget that as long as I live. That was the biggest thrill I had in baseball by far.

What about your biggest disappointment?

There were two. The first was when I was traded away from the Cubs.

Then what happened in '51, the home run by Bobby Thomson.

That's a real trivia question. Everybody knows who threw the ball — Ralph Branca. Everybody knows who hit the ball — Bobby Thomson. But very few people know who played left field that day. It was me.

I had the best seat in the house, the best view. Had the ball been hit in Ebbets Field I might have had a shot at it. But in the Polo Grounds it was only

279 down the line. It was about 20 feet off the line and it landed in the fourth or fifth row. When it left the bat I thought I might have a chance to catch it.

And a few years later, Bobby Thomson became a Milwaukee Brave. We were not only teammates, he was my roommate!

Bobby was a super guy. If it had to be hit, I'm glad he did it.

He broke his ankle in spring training with the Braves. Hank Aaron was supposed to go down for more seasoning, but Thomson broke his ankle so they gave the job to him. And the rest is history.

Did you enjoy your 17 years?

Definitely! I enjoyed every day.

Would you do it again?

You better believe it! I wouldn't do anything else. If I had a chance to be president of the United States I'd refuse it. My ambition was to be a baseball player.

I was very fortunate and I thank God I had the opportunity. I enjoyed every minute. I gave it all I had. I'm just grateful I was a major league ballplayer.

* * *

Andy Pafko holds another distinction, an important one to baseball card collectors. His is the number one card in the 1952 Topps set, the set that marked the dawning of the modern era of baseball cards. It was a large set, both in size and number, and it was the first set to have a colored team logo on the front and previous season and career statistics on the back.

But 1952 was eons before anyone dreamed of specially designed card boxes or plastic sheets in which to store them. No one thought in terms of "Mint" or "Near Mint." The true collectors took care of their cards, of course, but they did it the best way they could. Shoe boxes were a popular storage facility, but still they were shuffled about and bounced around, so, in an effort to hold them in place, the ever-popular rubber band was utilized.

As a result, the top card, card number one, usually ended up with a rubber band crease across the front. Because of this, all of the early number one's are valued above that of others of similar renown in the same set. The combination of Andy's popularity and his strategic position in this landmark set makes this card one of the most expensive in the card collecting hobby.

PLAYERS WITH MORE HOME RUNS THAN STRIKEOUTS IN ONE SEASON
(Minimum 35 home runs)

Year	Player, team	HR	SO
1922	Ken Williams, St Louis (AL)	39	31
1929	Mel Ott, New York (NL)	42	38
1930	Al Simmons, Philadelphia (AL)	36	34
1934	Lou Gehrig, New York (AL)	49	31
1936	Gehrig	49	46
1937	Joe DiMaggio, New York (AL)	46	37
1941	Ted Williams, Boston (AL)	37	27
1947	Johnny Mize, New York (NL)	51	42
	Willard Marshall, New York (NL)	36	30
1948	Mize	40	37
	J. DiMaggio	39	30
	Stan Musial, St. Louis (NL)	39	34
1950	ANDY PAFKO, Chicago (NL)	36	32
1953	Ted Kluszewski, Cincinnati	40	34
1954	Kluszewski	49	35
1955	Kluszewski	47	40
1956	Kluszewski	35	31

ANDREW (HANDY ANDY, PRUSCHKA) PAFKO
Born February 25, 1921, Boyceville, WI
Ht. 6'   Wt. 190   Batted and Threw Right

Year	Team	G	AB	R	H	2B	3B	HR	RBI	SB	BA	SA
1943	ChiN	13	58	7	22	3	0	0	10	1	.379	.431
1944		128	469	47	126	16	2	6	62	2	.269	.350
1945		144	534	64	159	24	12	12	110	5	.298	.455
1946		65	234	18	66	6	4	3	39	4	.282	.380
1947		129	513	68	155	25	7	13	66	4	.302	.454
1948		142	548	82	171	30	2	26	101	3	.312	.516
1949		144	519	79	146	19	2	18	69	4	.281	.449
1950		146	514	95	156	24	8	36	92	4	.304	.591
1951	ChiN	49	178	26	47	5	3	12	35	1	.264	.528
	BrkN	84	277	42	69	11	0	18	58	1	.249	.484

Year	Team	G	AB	R	H	2B	3B	HR	RBI	SB	BA	SA
1952	BrkN	150	551	76	158	17	5	19	85	4	.287	.439
1953	MilN	140	516	70	153	23	4	17	72	2	.297	.455
1954		138	510	61	146	22	4	14	69	1	.286	.427
1955		86	252	29	67	3	5	5	34	1	.266	.377
1956		45	93	15	24	5	0	2	9	0	.258	.376
1957		83	220	31	61	6	1	8	27	1	.277	.423
1958		95	164	17	39	7	1	3	23	0	.238	.348
1959		71	142	17	31	8	2	1	15	0	.218	.324
17 years		1852	6292	844	1796	264	62	213	976	38	.285	.449

World Series

Year	Team	G	AB	R	H	2B	3B	HR	RBI	SB	BA	SA
1945	ChiN	7	28	5	6	2	1	0	2	0	.214	.357
1952	BrkN	7	21	0	4	0	0	0	2	0	.190	.190
1957	MilN	6	14	1	3	0	0	0	0	0	.214	.214
1958		4	9	0	3	1	0	0	1	0	.333	.444
4 years		24	72	6	16	3	1	0	5	0	.222	.292

All-Star Game

Year	League	G	AB	R	H	2B	3B	HR	RBI	SB	BA	SA
1947	National	1	2	0	1	0	0	0	0	0	.500	.500
1948		1	2	0	0	0	0	0	0	0	.000	.000
1949		1	2	0	1	0	0	0	0	0	.500	.500
1950		1	4	0	2	0	0	0	0	0	.500	.500
4 years		4	10	0	4	0	0	0	0	0	.400	.400

MEL PARNELL

Mel Parnell (George Brace photograph).

The Fenway Southpaw
AL All-Star 1949, 1951

"If someone's not satisfied, it's his own fault."
— Mel Parnell

Here is a Red Sox pitching quiz:

1. Who was the last American League pitcher to win 25 games in a 154-game schedule? (The AL schedule went to 162 games in 1961.)
2. Who was the first Red Sox southpaw to win 20 games since Lefty Grove in 1935?
3. For that matter, who was the *last* Red Sox lefty, to the present time, to win 20 games?
4. Who among left-handers has the most 20-win seasons in a Red Sox uniform? This one's tricky — there's a three-way tie, but only one of them pitched in the live-ball era (and one pitched before Fenway Park was built).
5. And, finally, who is the only Red Sox left-hander, other than Grove, to ever lead the AL in ERA in the live-ball era?

Here are the answers:

1. Mel Parnell won 25 games in 1949.
2. Mel Parnell, 1949.
3. Mel Parnell won 21 games in 1953.
4. The three are tied with two 20-win seasons apiece: Mel Parnell, 1949 and 1953; Babe Ruth, 1916 and 1917; and Jesse Tannehill, 1904 and 1905, when the team played at the old Huntington Avenue Grounds. Only one of Grove's eight 20-win seasons came as a member of the Red Sox.
5. Mel Parnell, with 2.77 in 1949.

Take a look at Parnell's 1949 record at the end of this chapter. He was the best pitcher in baseball that year.

But how good was he, other than that season?

There were five future Hall of Fame pitchers whose careers roughly coincided with Parnell's. They, along with Mel, are in the first table on page 126, which gives the following information: (1) Career Win-Loss Percentage for each man, (2) the Win-Loss Percentage of his team(s) during his career, (3) the difference between his percentage and his team's, and (4) the percent better his Win-Loss Percentage was better than that of his team(s).

The table at bottom of page 126 concerns ERA, and the same four bits of revelation are included.

And the table at top of page 127 lists all the major league pitchers who won 90 or more games between 1948 and 1953. Also included are their Win-Loss Percentage and ERA for this six-year period. (We could build a pitching staff around these ten guys.)

In reading these tables, please remember that Mel Parnell threw left-handed and that his home field was Fenway Park, the home of the Green Monster.

Due to World War II early and a bad elbow late, Mel was only in the majors for ten years. All were with Boston. For his career, he was 125-73 and his .621 percentage ranks him 37th among all hurlers with 100 wins since 1900.

These figures are impressive, but the most dazzling of all is his record at home. At Fenway, the graveyard of left-handers, Mel won 70 games and lost only 30! For those of you without a computer handy, that's a winning percentage of .700.

In both 1948 and '49, the Bosox were a good team. An excellent team. They finished second both years, losing a sudden-death play-off to Cleveland in '48 and being nosed out by the Yankees on the last day of the '49 season.

But other than these two years, they were basically a middle-of-the-pack outfit throughout Mel's career.

So what we have is a left-handed pitcher pitching in the worst ballpark in the world for left-handers who won 62 percent of his games for a team that, 80 percent of the time he was there, finished third through sixth.

Even today, 40 years after he threw his last pitch, no Red Sox lefty has ever won more games than Mel Parnell, in a season or in a career.

One of the favorite speculations of baseball fans through the years has been what would Ted Williams have accomplished if he had played in Yankee Stadium and what would Joe DiMaggio have done if he had played in Fenway Park. Here's a proposed trade, retroactive to, say, April 1, 1947: Ted Williams and Mel Parnell for Joe DiMaggio and Allie Reynolds.

Until the advent of the first time machine, though, we'll have to settle for history as it was.

You lost three years to the service in World War II. You had gone 16-9, 1.59 with Canton in the Mid-Atlantic League in 1942, then spent '43, '44, and '45 with Uncle Sam. Do you think you'd have come to the major leagues sooner if not for that?

Mel Parnell: I think so, because during the time I was in the service I was pitching for a military team and Hugh Mulcahy, who was a pitcher for the Philadelphia Phillies, wanted to know if I could get a release from the Red Sox. He said he could get me a very healthy contract with the Phillies. So that, of course, made me feel that I was probably ready at that time.

In 1949, you were the best pitcher in baseball. Do you think you would have won the Cy Young Award if it had been given then?

I think I would have had a very good chance, yes. I think my stats proved to make me very much eligible for it. I think I could have won it at that time.

Why were you so successful in Fenway Park?

I think one reason for my success was keeping the ball in tight on right-handed hitters. Naturally, every right-handed hitter going into Fenway Park had one thing in mind: the left field wall. I thought that by keeping the ball in tight on 'em, and moving the ball—breaking pitches in most cases—they were swinging with their elbows close to the body and not with arms extended. Of course, in keeping the elbows close to the body, they were sacrificing power.

Another thing, too, I felt by doing this the left field wall didn't bother me one bit. I felt I could protect myself against that left field wall. The one thing I couldn't protect myself against at Fenway Park was the lack of foul territory. There were balls going into the seats that in other ballparks were outs. To me, that is the *biggest* detriment to pitching in Fenway Park. And it's certainly an asset to hitting. I felt it meant at least 15 to 20 points to a hitter's average in that ballpark.

The 1949 pennant race: At the end of the season, the Red Sox were throwing you and Ellis Kinder every time they could.

Yeah. Ellis and I were in the bullpen or in the game the last 19 days of the season and we threw on each of the 19 days.

Did this cost you the pennant?

I think it probably took something out of us, really. You know, throwing constantly for 19 days, we were a little tired. I lost something like 25 pounds during the season. When I got home, my family doctor told me when he saw me, "Go someplace and get lost. You need some rest."

We didn't have the depth in the bullpen and we didn't have the real outstanding reliever in the bullpen, like a Joe Page of the Yankees. We had a chance to get a fellow that I thought could have been very helpful to us, but the Red Sox didn't make the deal for some reason. Max Surkont — he was being offered and we felt pretty much that if we had a Max Surkont in our bullpen, we could have been the winning ballclub that year.

He was a very good pitcher and at that time you could get enough out of him to do a good relief role. He was with the White Sox at the time. For some reason, Joe Cronin didn't want to make the deal. As a team, we felt that he could have been a difference.

Tell us about a few of your teammates. Ellis Kinder — he was a long way from being a young man when he joined the Red Sox.

That's right. He was an exceptional guy. Ellis had what we called a rubber arm, a guy who could go out and throw every day. He had one of the best change-ups ever in baseball and this made him very effective. He was a highly competitive fellow.

He was the first pitcher to have both a 20-win season and a 20-save season.

Yeah. He passed away — he had a heart attack quite a few years ago. He kind of lived on the wild side pretty much but he would come out and give you 110 percent every time. Every time he walked to the mound, you had a challenge.

Your center fielder, Dom DiMaggio, certainly didn't get the press that Joe did, but a lot of people say he was a better fielder. Was he?

Yeah. I thought he lived in the shadow of Joe. He was a great outfielder and, of course, where I stood on the mound I got to see many things that he was capable of doing.

Mel Parnell (courtesy of *The National Pastime*).

He covered a lot of left-center and right-center both and he was one of the best I've ever seen at coming in on a line drive and making a shoestring catch. He was the only guy that I could truthfully say could reach down and make the catch without breaking stride. Not too many can do that. Dom was just an excellent outfielder. He was an excellent lead-off man, also.

He was a .300 hitter. Is he a candidate for the Hall of Fame in your mind?

In my mind, yes. Definitely. He was a great ballplayer. Like you said, he just didn't get the press that his brother got. Everything was "Joe" and he was always "Joe's little brother," you know, not "Dominic."

What about Johnny Pesky?

Johnny was a good hitter. He had *great* bat control and as a number two hitter, he and Dominic, I would say, were the best one-two punch in baseball. Dominic would get on and Pesky could move him over to third base very easily. Sometimes he bunted and drew the third baseman in and Dominic would just continue going all the way to third base. Of course, when they got wise to that, Johnny'd start doing other things. But Johnny had great bat control and I thought he was a very excellent hitter although he didn't go for the long ball. He just tried to pick his spots and he was very good in doing that.

Those three guys who followed them had an awful lot of runners on base with those two guys at the top of the order.

They sure did.

What about one of those guys: Vern Stephens. If there was ever a hitter made for Fenway Park, it was him.

He certainly was. Vern was very strong from the waist up. He had that open stance and more or less stepped in the bucket, as we called it. But he was so strong through the upper part of his body that he was able to compensate for that bucket stance that he had. Fenway Park was an ideal place for Vern.

How was he as a shortstop?

Adequate, very adequate. I wouldn't say he was the most outstanding shortstop, but he was adequate. He could make the plays for you. I think Vern probably would have been a better third baseman than a shortstop.

Walt Dropo may have had the best rookie year ever. What happened after that?

Walt was a big, free-swinging guy and, as you mentioned before, he got a lot of guys on base in front of him and he was able to be very productive that year. After that, I think the pitchers probably caught on to Walt a little bit and pitched him a little differently.

In 1953, you had your second 20-win season and Mickey McDermott had 18 wins. Both of you were left-handed. How did McDermott handle Fenway, did he pitch the same way you did?

He and I were roommates and I constantly tried to drive it into his head that he had to pitch inside in Fenway and I think Mickey started doing that and had a little better success.

He had a reputation as being sort of a loose horse.

Yes, he was. Very loose (Laughs) (Joe) McCarthy (Red Sox manager) first roomed me with him and told me to be a father to him, but that was kind of hard to do 'cause we had completely different personalities. He was very loose and I was very conservative, but I did my best with him and to this day we're very good friends and appreciative of each other.

I guess he's included among those guys who wasted his talent.

He had a million dollars worth of ability. He had one of the best arms that I've ever seen. I recall in spring training one time, in warming up on the sidelines and seeing this little skinny kid come up on the side of me and get on the mound and call for a catcher and start throwing. All I could hear was that catcher's glove exploding, so I stopped throwing and started watching him. I thought he was the bat boy at first. (Laughs) He was a little, scrawny kid, but had a *great* arm. The best I've ever seen, really. This kid could really throw. He wasn't a bad hitter, either.

The Sox had several good left-handers. Besides you and McDermott, there was Chuck Stobbs, another kid.

Chuck was a good pitcher. He was a pretty heady guy and knew how to pitch. He didn't just rear back and fire the ball. He had intentions with each and every pitch.

In '53, you shut out the Yankees four times.

I beat 'em five times and shut 'em out four. They were tough but I think the thing that got to me was Casey Stengel. In years prior to that year I had pretty good success against the Yankees and Casey kept switching the lineup around. I beat his all right-handed lineup, then he went to an all left-handed lineup and I beat them, so he went back to the right. He'd always keep yelling at me, "You don't have any right to beat us!" That gave me a little more incentive to go a little harder against the Yankees.

We had such a great rivalry. We hated each other on the field but we had great respect for each other off the field.

The Red Sox were usually a little short. The Yankees were always on top and you were always down around third or fourth. What did you lack?

We were a step slower than they were in the field. They had a little more team speed than we did.

And, again, the guy I mentioned before: Joe Page in the bullpen. Had we had a good stopper like that, I think it could have been a different story.

They did have a little more speed than we had, and they had a little more depth than we had, too. They had those big outfielders and every one of them could mash the ball out of the ballpark. We just didn't go that deep.

You came up with an elbow problem in 1954.

A nerve got caught between the bones in the elbow. I tore a muscle and the muscle put the nerve in between the bones. I had it operated on. The doctor told me I'd have to have two more operations to keep going 'cause I had spurs in the elbow as well. At that time, I figured it was a little late in the career for me, so it was about time to bow out. Had I been, say, 20 or 21 years old, I would have had it done, but at that time it was getting a little late.

Then, Mickey McDermott got traded over to Washington. In '54 he broke my arm. We were pitching against each other one night and planning to go to dinner after the game. He threw a fastball to me that took off and the ball sailed in on me and, trying to get away from it, it hit the ulna bone in my left arm and broke it. Then that set me back for quite a while.

I think, when that happened, Mickey was in more pain than I was. He came into the clubhouse and when I told him it was broken, I saw tears coming out of his eyes.

After that I was able to come back and then I pitched a no-hitter.

That was in 1956, your last season. Was that the best game you ever pitched?

I don't know if it was the best one. It was one of the best. It was a day when I could get my sinker right were I wanted it, just about, and everything pretty much fell in place for me, which has to happen for a pitcher to pitch a no-hitter. I had good stuff, I had great control of it, and I think that was the deciding factor in the outcome of that game.

Was that your biggest thrill?

It was. It's something that I think all pitchers dream of but you never expect it to happen.

I've heard so many pitchers say that they didn't know they were going for a no-hitter. I can't believe that. You have to know, 'cause if you aren't in mind of it the crowd reminds you of it as you get into the late innings — the seventh inning on, at least. With each out the outburst out of the crowd is a reminder to you. You're sitting in that ballpark and you're looking at the scoreboard, also, and the scoreboard indicates what's happened. I can't believe any pitcher that says he didn't know he was going for it. To me, that's a lot of hooey.

Who was the best player you saw?

I guess I'd have to say (Joe) DiMaggio. He was a threat every time he swung the bat.

I'd say the toughest hitter I ever pitched to, though, was Luke Appling. Luke was a guy that was easy to get two strikes on, but hard as hell to get the third one. When I saw Luke Appling it was at the end of his career and the beginning of mine. I thought he was very tough. He could get the bat on the ball. He was a good control hitter.

And Lou Boudreau was a tough hitter. Harvey Kuenn was also a tough hitter.

Who was the one best hitter you saw?

Ted Williams, without a doubt. Williams was the best hitter by far, and DiMaggio was a better outfielder than Ted, but not that much. Ted was a very underrated outfielder. He was a big, gangly type of guy that didn't look good going after the ball, but he got there and got it.

He played that left field wall better than anybody I've ever seen, Yastrzemski included. Carl played it very well, but I think Williams played it even better. It seems like he knew where every rib in that fence was and knew what kind of bounce you'd get off that wall.

The guy was amazing. He was the most perfect self-made man I've ever seen. Anything he encountered he did it to perfection.

Who was the best pitcher you saw?

Best pitcher. Well, I guess I'd have to go to (Bob) Feller. Allie Reynolds, too, was very tough. I thought maybe Feller may have been a little more consistent than Reynolds, but on certain days Reynolds could be as fast as anybody.

He was a late bloomer.

Yes, he was.

He pitched a no-hitter against me in New York one day, and, I tell you, it was the best stuff we had ever seen. He was just blowing the ball past us.

Consistently, I'd say probably Feller. As a matter of fact, that whole Cleveland staff at that time was tough. I would have to believe that was the best pitching staff ever in baseball. You had (Bob) Lemon, Feller, (Early) Wynn, (Mike) Garcia, then they picked up Art Houtteman from Detroit as a fifth starter. And they had the two guys in the bullpen, (Ray) Narleski and (Don) Mossi. And then they had Steve Gromek, also, who was a capable pitcher. He'd come in every now and then and shut the door on somebody.

And later Herb Score.

Yeah. I pitched against Herb quite a few times and he was quick but I thought Feller may have been just a little bit quicker than him. Of course, he was a little more deceptive hitting from the left-hand side of the plate against him.

I remember the first game I pitched against him. The fellows on the bench were telling me, before I went up to the plate, to be ready 'cause he was quick. So I was down on the handle of the bat and the first pitch he threw me, before I even got around on it, I could hear the "pop" in the catcher's mitt. (Laughs) I thought, "Gee, they didn't say this guy was *this* quick." So I opened up my stance and on the next pitch he threw the fast ball again and I just threw the bat out in front of the ball and made contact. The ball went off the left field wall. I got a double. He supplied the power. I didn't. (Laughs)

Cleveland had so many good pitchers year after year. They got guys like Wynn, who was just another pitcher until the Indians got him. Mel Harder was their pitching coach. With all the pitching that Cleveland developed, does he belong in the Hall of Fame?

I would say he does. I thought he was an outstanding individual, as well as a pitcher. He certainly does deserve that recognition because the guy was a great one. No doubt about it. And he's one of the finest fellows you'll ever meet. He's a great guy.

I occasionally see him at baseball functions and I'm very happy to see him 'cause I enjoy talking with him. Just a pleasant fellow.

You managed in the minors for several years. Did you enjoy that?

Not really. Neil Mahoney, the farm director for the Red Sox, talked me into managing.

I managed here in New Orleans the last year they had a ballclub here. The mayor called me in and asked me to take over the ballclub and try and get things going, but they were in bad financial straits and they didn't have any talent. They were an independent and I got a lot of guys out of retirement and got 'em to come play with us. We were doing a hell of a job, we were leading the league for a while 'til they started breaking down physically. (Laughs) Then things got a little though.

Twig Rickey saved me, here in New Orleans, 'cause he sent me a lot of ballplayers to fill in — guys that really weren't ready for Double-A baseball but guys that I could put a uniform on and play with.

Then, after that, Neil Mahoney talked me into managing for the Red Sox and I went out to Alpine, Texas, in the Sophomore League. I had a bunch of their bonus kids out there. Then the next year I went to York, Pennsylvania, and then the year after that I went up to Seattle.

But after Seattle I had enough of it. I told Mahoney I was quitting. He said, "You can't do that." I said, "The hell I can't. I don't want to do it. I don't enjoy it." (Laughs) So I quit that and Curt Gowdy called me and I worked with him broadcasting Red Sox ballgames.

How long did you do that?

I was with the Red Sox four years broadcasting, then I went over to Chicago. I had a pretty good deal over there, but I didn't like the setup in Chicago. The living conditions there weren't favorable for my family, so — I had a two-year contract — after the first year I asked to get out of the contract. They told me, "You can't. You've got another year to go." We debated for quite a while and finally I got 'em to the point where, if I recommended somebody that would meet their approval, they'd let me out. So I got Billy Pierce — they agreed to accept him and I got out of the contract.

Then they fired Billy at the end of his first year.

He was a heck of a pitcher.

Yes, he was. A pretty good one.

I think they accepted him with the expectation that he'd be a real big draw there in Chicago, 'cause at that time the Cubs were coming on a little strong and (it was) getting a little competitive between the two teams.

It's been 50 years since you began playing professional baseball. There's been a lot of changes in the game — in the attitudes and the way it's played and a lot of things.

In the paychecks, too. (Laughs)

A lot different in the paychecks. What do you think is the biggest difference, other than that?

In the actual play, I think the biggest change came in the pitching. They'll tell the starting pitcher to "go out and give me five or six innings, then I can bring somebody else along" and so forth, where we didn't have that luxury of just working five or six innings. We had to go as far as we could. If you couldn't go the distance, in most cases they frowned on your ability and down you went to the minors.

But today, it's altogether different. They've got the middle reliever and the short reliever and all that stuff, where we just had relievers. You went as far as you could and if someone came on it was usually some guy that had been a starter and they'd just shoved him out in the bullpen. He didn't have the experience of being just one way, of being a one-inning or two-inning or three-inning pitcher like they're doing today.

The money — of course the effect of television has increased that considerably. I think it's getting to the point now where they're killing the goose laying the golden egg. Something's going to have to happen real soon.

I saw in the paper where one team's salary went up eight million since last year. You know, they keep doing that kind of stuff and somebody's gonna be on the outside looking in. That's gotta turn that turnstile a lot of times to make that up. If that ballclub comes up with a bad year now, they're gonna *really* hurt.

And the Red Sox, too, giving (Roger) Clemens all that money. They upped their payroll considerably, too, and they've got a small ballpark where they're gonna be limited in attendance. They can wind up hurting, too, if they come up with a bad year.

I hope they succeed, but it's gonna be a little tight, I'm sure.

Did you save souvenirs from your career?

Some. Not too much. I wish I had saved more. When you're playing, you're concentrating on what you're doing. You're not worrying about all that souvenir stuff. You're looking for your bread-and-butter. (Laughs)

Do you receive much fan mail today?

Yeah, quite a bit. Every day I get something in the mail.

Had you played in New York, you may have ruled the world, but you were a big favorite in Boston. I imagine you're still very popular in that area.

Yes. It makes me feel good to go up and to be recognized and remembered. But, like you mentioned, in New York and Los Angeles they got *most* of the publicity.

Boston was good baseball country, though. We pretty much ran the Braves out of town there. Their ballpark wasn't too inviting to the fans, where ours was. And our ballclub was just a little bit better than theirs was and eventually they decided to pull out to Milwaukee, which was a good deal on their part. Of course, that left us the sole club there and the enthusiasm just kept building up and building up. It was just a good town to play in.

We had a lot of press there that was fighting for stories and with that they were doing a lot of ripping and everything. One in particular was Dave Egan — *no* one was good in his opinion: Ted Williams was a lousy hitter, Rocky Marciano was a lousy heavyweight, Casey Stengel was a lousy manager. (Laughs) Everybody that had success he criticized, but he claimed he did that for one sole reason and that was to sell newspapers. And that he did.

Is your fan mail mostly autograph requests?

Yeah. I get a lot of cards from kids, which I sign and send back to 'em. A lot of guys won't sign 'em — they want to be paid for it. But I was a kid once and I collected 'em and I know just how these kids feel, so I sign 'em and send 'em back to 'em. I return every one I get.

If you went back 50 years, would you be a professional baseball player again?

I certainly would and I'd recommend it for any kid coming up today that has the ability. To me, it's a great life. You do a lot of traveling, you meet a lot of good people, you live in the best places. What more can you ask in life? I think it's a great life and I have to recommend it for every kid that has the ability.

What about regrets?

The only thing I regret is the salaries weren't as good then as they are now. (Laughs)

I'm very much satisfied with the way my career went. I have no complaints whatsoever. Truthfully, I went farther than I thought I would. Coming in to professional baseball early you don't expect to have a real outstanding career, although you're trying and doing everything that you can. But every brick has to fall in the right place to more or less have that great career. You have to avoid injury, for one thing.

I truthfully don't regret anything that happened. I was really thrilled at the whole outcome of it.

If someone's not satisfied, it's his own fault. Apparently he didn't apply himself enough or whatever. Or didn't that take care of himself. There can be many factors, I guess, that can cause 'em to be disenchanted with the outcome.

I think a young man going in to baseball should grade his progress over his first three years to determine whether he's gonna stay or get out, because if he's not making progress it's best to get out. You can be out in some other endeavor building up security.

	W-L Pct	Team W-L Pct	Diff.	%
MEL PARNELL	.621	.554	+.067	12.1
Robin Roberts	.539	.485	+.054	11.1
Warren Spahn	.597	.543	+.054	9.9
Bob Feller	.621	.568	+.053	9.3
Bob Lemon	.618	.574	+.044	7.7
Early Wynn	.551	.533	+.018	3.4

	ERA	Team ERA	Diff.	%
MEL PARNELL	3.50	4.30	-.53	13.2
Warren Spahn	3.09	3.60	-.51	14.2

	ERA	Team ERA	Diff.	%
Bob Feller	3.25	3.68	-.43	11.7
Robin Roberts	3.41	3.80	-.39	10.3
Bob Lemon	3.23	3.46	-.23	6.6
Early Wynn	3.54	3.68	-.14	3.8

	W-L	PCT	ERA
Bob Lemon	125-75	.625	3.17
Warren Spahn	116-83	.583	3.00
Robin Roberts	114-73	.610	2.99
Vic Raschi	111-48	.698	3.43
MEL PARNELL	109-56	.642	3.20
Ed Lopat	97-47	.674	3.06
Early Wynn	97-71	.577	3.79
Larry Jansen	97-79	.551	3.59
Bob Feller	91-68	.572	3.71
Preacher Roe	90-33	.732	3.20

MELVIN LLOYD (DUSTY) PARNELL
Born June 13, 1922, New Orleans, LA
Ht. 6'   Wt. 180   Batted and Threw Left

Year	Team	G	IP	W	L	PCT	H	BB	SO	SHO	SV	ERA
1947	BosA	15	50.2	2	3	.400	60	27	23	0	0	6.39
1948		35	212	15	8	.652	205	90	77	1	0	3.14
1949		39	295.1*	25*	7	.781	258	134	122	4	2	2.77*
1950		40	249	18	10	.643	244	106	93	2	3	3.61
1951		36	221	18	11	.621	229	77	77	3	2	3.26
1952		33	214	12	12	.500	207	89	107	3	2	3.62
1953		38	241	21	8	.724	217	116*	136	5	0	3.06
1954		19	92.1	3	7	.300	104	35	28	1	0	3.70
1955		13	46	2	3	.400	62	25	18	0	1	7.83
1956		21	131.1	7	6	.538	129	59	41	1	0	3.77
10 years		289	1752.2	123	75	.621	1715	758	732	20	10	3.50

All-Star Game

Year	League	ST	IP	H	R	ER	BB	SO	ERA
1949	American	1	1	3	3	3	1	1	27.00
1951			1	3	1	1	0	1	9.00
2 years		1	2	6	4	4	1	2	18.00

*Led league (According to the rules of the day, Mel's ERA in 1949 led the league. New reference books have applied new rules to older stats and have taken the leadership away from him.)

BILL RIGNEY

Bill Rigney, the Giants' first manager in San Francisco (courtesy of San Francisco Giants).

Full Circle
NL All-Star 1948

"To me there's a difference in the Hall of Fame. Is he a Hall of Famer or was he just a good player?"
— Bill Rigney

Bill Rigney has been in baseball for over a half century and has gotten nowhere. Back in 1938, fresh out of high school, he signed with the hometown Oakland organization. And that's where he finds himself today — with the hometown Oakland organization.

A few things happened in the intervening years, though, to add a little variety to his resumé: five years in the minors; three years in the service; eight years in the majors with the Giants, during which time he appeared in both a World Series and an All-Star Game and contributed substantially to his team's major league home run record; back to the minors as a playing manager for two years; then 18 years as a major league manager.

In 1955, he led the Minneapolis Millers to the American Association championship and in 1956 he replaced his former manager, the legendary Leo Durocher, as the Giants' skipper and he remained at the team's helm when the franchise moved to San Francisco in 1958.

He had a couple of good teams there in '58 and '59, finishing third both years. The '59 pennant race was a particularly exciting one: it went into the last week with three teams — the Giants, Dodgers, and Braves — within two games of each other.

San Francisco tried to do it with a four-man rotation, while Los Angeles and Milwaukee were going with five (and occasionally six) starters. The workload finally took its toll as the Giants faded to finish three games behind the tied Braves and Dodgers. (L.A. won a play-off, two games to none.)

Nineteen sixty came with predictions of a Giants' pennant, but '59 Rookie-of-the-Year Willie McCovey fell victim to the sophomore jinx and ace lefty Johnny Antonelli suddenly became ineffective. Slightly more than a third of the way into the season the Giants were in second place, only two-and-a-half games back, when the decision was made to change managers — Rig was fired. San Francisco played sub-.500 the rest of the way and dropped to fifth.

The next season, 1961, expansion began and Bill was hired by Gene Autry to guide the fledgling Los Angeles Angels. In the ten-team league, he led them to an eighth-place finish, actually finishing ahead of an established team in addition to beating out the other expansion franchise.

Then, in '62, he took the Angels to the quickest first division finish ever for an expansion team. He led a collection of cast-offs, journeymen, and unproven youngsters to an 86-76 record, ten games behind the World Champion Yankees (who, by the way, beat his old Giants, with the nucleus he left behind, in the Series).

He remained as the Angels' skipper through their move to Anaheim (and became the first manager to ever shift cities with two different clubs) and in 1970 he moved on to Minnesota, where he won the West Division title.

After leaving the Twins, he returned to pilot the Giants for one more year (1976) and since has scouted and been an announcer and an executive. That's where he is now: full-circle back to Oakland. It's a different franchise in a higher league, but it's home.

His leadership abilities and eye for talent are still strong and he's still contributing to baseball in his 70s.

You're from Alameda and originally signed with the Oakland Oaks out of high school. After five minor league seasons, you went in the service. Did you play ball there and were there many professional players?

Bill Rigney: Yeah, but there weren't many professionals. I was at pre-flight school so there was only about 1,500 cadets and a couple hundred officers. I was an enlisted man and Ray Scarborough was there, who later pitched for the Washington Senators, and Bill Wight, who later pitched for the Yankees and White Sox, and there was a third baseman from the San Francisco Seals named Ray Perry, but those were about the only professional players we had. Charlie Gehringer was there as a manager — he was stationed there in, I think, '43 — and he played about two or three games. There were a few officers that had played baseball but not professionally.

Did you have a good team?

Oh, yeah. We had a fine team. Any team that had Wight on it was a good team.

I remember a game against some Army team. I think we played 16 innings and he pitched the whole game and struck out 26. I hit a home run in the sixteenth inning to win it, 4-to-3 or something like that.

When you came out of the service you went straight to the Giants. When did they acquire you?

They bought me while I was in the service — about '43, I think.

In '47 you hit 17 home runs. That was more than you had hit in your entire life. What happened?

I guess my roommate had a little influence on me — Johnny Mize. He hit 51 that year. It seems like everybody got into the act.

But I think the main thing was Ernie Lombardi was on that team and, having been from Oakland, he kind of took a liking to me. I didn't know Lom very well, but I knew of him and I'd met him before. He gave me some tips about hitting in the Polo Grounds. The lines were short. He said, "You ought to become a pull hitter here because you can get the best of it because you can reach the seats easy."

So he worked with me in the spring and when I finally got a chance to play everything worked fine. Everybody had good years hitting home runs. (1947 was the year the Giants set a new team home run record with 221.)

Your pitchers evidently didn't have good seasons.

No. Larry Jansen as a rookie did. He was 21 and five. He was about the *only* thing we had. We couldn't beat you very often 2-to-1 but we could beat you 8-to-7.

The next year you were selected for the All-Star Game. You must have been doing awfully well at mid-season.

Well, not really. I think I was hitting .280 or something like that but I got in on the last second. Leo (Durocher) had come over to manage the club — from Brooklyn — and the (All-Star) teams had been picked. I've got to be fairly honest about this. I wasn't on the team but (Eddie) Stanky broke his leg on Sunday prior to the All-Star Game. Leo picked me to take his place.

Does that rank up there with your biggest thrills?

That was certainly one of them. Being on the Giants in 1951 was certainly a thrill — you don't ever forget those kind of years when the team did so many things so well in the last half of the season.

What do you remember about that pennant race?

We were out 13 games and we won 16 in a row and we closed the gap quite a bit then, but we still had to go on a western trip when we were seven or eight games back. On that trip, of the 12 or 13 games, we won 11 or 12. I think we only lost one game. Now that closed it down to about one or two (games out).

I remember the last series in Boston so well. On Saturday, (Sal) Maglie beat Boston 3-to-2, and on Sunday, Jansen beat Boston 3-to-2. Those were two money games we *had* to have and we won 'em' both.

Then we won the first game of the play-offs and then Clem Labine shut us out the second game. *Years* later I remember talking to Bobby (Thomson) and he said, "You know, it was kinda funny, wasn't it, Rig? I came off that diamond (after game two) and here we were going to play 157 (games) and nothing had been decided yet."

Where were you when he hit the home run?

I had pinch-hit in the eighth inning. Stanky had come back about the fifth or something and said, "The big guy's (Don Newcombe) losing a little bit. If we can stay close, we can get him."

So I went up to pinch-hit in the eighth inning — leading off the eighth — and the first pitch he threw me was just a rocket! Stanky was in the on-deck circle and I kind of backed off and looked at him and said, "Yeah, it looks like he's lost a lot." (Laughs) Well, he struck out the side in the eighth inning. He struck me out — I hit for (Wes) Westrum, I think — and he struck out a pinch-hitter for the pitcher and then he struck out Stanky. But that was it. It all must have gone right then.

But then (Don) Mueller broke his leg on (Whitey) Lockman's double off the wall in left field. Mueller slid into third base and broke a bone in his foot. I helped carry him off because I was already out of the game. I was in the clubhouse when Bobby hit the home run.

Bill Rigney (courtesy of *The National Pastime*).

So you missed it?

Oh, no, I saw it. You could see it from the clubhouse. In the Polo Grounds the windows in center field let you look out on the field.

The scoreboards hung over the lower deck and Bobby just hit a hard sinker and it hit some little kid right in the belly right alongside the foul pole.

You mentioned Leo Durocher. Does he belong in the Hall of Fame?

It's hard for me to say. As a manager, I think he does. I don't know if the consideration of his associations with the gamblers in '47 when he was suspended has an effect.

Let me put it this way: I really enjoyed playing for him. He was a motivator. One thing I remember about Leo, if he had a club that had a chance to win he could win with it and if he had a club that was going to be a second division club he might have lost a little interest. But as far as managing the game, I think we all learned from him, all of us that went on to be managers.

I know his name has come up a lot for the Hall and each time he seems to just miss it in that veterans division. I'm sure Buzzie (Bavasi) has been trying to get him in; he's on that committee. (Durocher was finally elected to the Hall of Fame in 1994.)

Did you style your managing after him?

Not really, but I learned a lot because when (Al) Dark and Stanky came over to the club I knew I wasn't going to be a regular player anymore. I'd been a regular player in '48 and '49 and then they came over in '50; well that meant that I *wasn't* going to have a lot of playing time. I had never thought about managing or what I was going to do when I couldn't play anymore and then I guess those years of sitting on the bench as a part-time player I started to think about what the future might bring. The more I thought about it the more managing seemed likely. I didn't dream — I later found this out — that Carl Hubbell, who was the farm director, had hoped that, when I *was* through, I would go managing because he thought that I should.

So in '51 and '52 and '53, I started thinking about that way and I watched everybody — all the managers. Being right there watching Leo and how he would gamble at the right time, I certainly learned a lot.

There were six managers off that one Giant club. There was Lockman and Westrum and Dark and Stanky and Herman Franks and myself. Franks was coaching then.

Let me ask you about some of the guys you played with and managed. Alvin Dark was a winning ballplayer. Was he a Hall of Fame-caliber player?

I don't think so. To me there's a difference in the Hall of Fame. Is he a Hall of Famer or was he just a good player? To me, Alvin Dark was a good player and he was certainly a fine offensive shortstop, maybe not the greatest-looking shortstop but he certainly got the job done as well as anybody. I don't think he was a Hall of Famer.

You managed Orlando Cepeda. A lot of people think he's Hall of Fame quality.

I think he would be in that area. His stats were certainly Hall of Fame stats, there's no doubt about that, but whether or not his off-the-field performance is going to enter into that, I can't say. But he certainly has all the qualifications to find a place in the Hall of Fame, I think.

This brings up a question. You've mentioned it with both Cepeda and Durocher: the off-the-field things. It says in the Hall of Fame requirements that a candidate has to be a tribute to the game and an upstanding citizen, etc. This has kept Joe Jackson out, yet most people say that Pete Rose, who is not a pillar of the community, will make it into the Hall. Do you have an opinion?

Well, yes. I'm embarrassed. Pete Rose is an embarrassment for me, for the game of baseball, and I'm embarrassed for him. That's about as much as I can tell you about whether Pete Rose should go into the Hall of Fame or not.

Tell us about Sal Maglie.

Oh, he was a fine money pitcher and when you played behind guys like Maglie and Jansen you knew every time they went out there you had a chance to win. They were always ready to pitch and they were solid citizens with a great deal of character and men that were fun to be on the same club with.

Maglie missed several years over the Mexican League.

He was gone in '46, '47, '48 and came back in '49 or '50. He said later that when he went down there he learned a lot about pitching. I guess that just came through experience. He might have learned the same thing in the National League.

I guess he was in his early 30s when he got back.

Yeah, right.

Larry Jansen — he was also not too young when he made it to the majors. When I was a boy, he always seemed to have a spotless reputation. Was he as good as he seemed?

Absolutely. He was a marvelous man. You know, he and Elaine had, I think, nine kids. It was nice to see him at this old-timers' game. He came down to play in the A's and Giants old-timers' game and Elaine was there and, by George, she looked just the same as she looked when we were playing in New York.

Larry, yes, I'd have to put him as a solid citizen.

There were a couple of young men whom you managed with the Angels who looked like they could be world-beaters: Ken McBride and Dean Chance.

They were a little bit different. McBride had a marvelous curveball and was a *really* good competitor. Maybe not the greatest stuff in the world, but he kept you around the ballgame all the time. He never got you far away. He made every start, but he came up with a little arm trouble later on in his career. For those early years he was a *very* good pitcher for us.

Of course, the other guy (Chance) I thought was the best right arm that I'd ever managed. Nineteen sixty-four, I guess it was, he pitched four times against the Yankees and gave 'em one run. He should have been better. He had a *marvelous*, just a *great* arm! Solid. As a matter of fact, I had him in the bullpen originally and it was kind of nice to have him down there. Your starter'd go seven innings and you'd bring him in and he'd strike out four of the six, but we knew eventually he had to be a starting pitcher because there was just too much ability to leave down there.

I just thought he was like a comet — he came fast and he left fast. With all the ability he had and as young as he was — he was real young when we drafted him from Baltimore — it just seemed like there was an awful lot of good stuff that never got it all done.

It was said once that he did little off-season conditioning and came to spring training out of shape.

He lived in a farming community and we never looked into what was going on in the off-season. I think that's a lot different from the modern player. He (the modern player) does a lot of things now to make sure that he doesn't get that way (out of shape). But Dean was a big kid with, like I say, the *best* right arm I'd ever managed — I didn't manage (Juan) Marichal — other than Sam Jones.

Bo Belinsky.

(Laughs) Bo liked the night life and I think Bo would have liked to pitch and then not show up until it was his turn to pitch again. But his no-hitter was a solid no-hitter, there's no doubt about that. He should have been better, too. He had enough equipment to be a lot better. There were just too many distractions for both he and Dean. Being in Hollywood and the movie industry all around him and then the no-hitter, I think his values got kind of side-tracked in some directions, but his equipment was good enough. I don't think he won 20 games (in his career), did he? (Yes, 28-51 in eight years.)

Off the field was important to both of those young men and if they'd have put that much importance on the field I think both of 'em would have been solid performers for quite a while. They just didn't last long enough, that's all. Dean pitched from '62, then went to Minnesota, and was gone by, what, '70? (Actually from the end of '61 through '71, he was 128-115, 2.92.)

So if these boys had come up in Kansas City or somewhere with a little less action, it may have benefited them?

Who knows. You can't look back and say it would have been different had they been here or there. I know they both enjoyed their time in the major leagues, let me put it that way. (Laughs)

Sam Jones.

Sam was just a *marvelous* pitcher and a good competitor and probably had the best curveball that we'd seen in the National League in years and years. He was a delightful guy, kind of quiet, never said boo. I really enjoyed managing him.

Why didn't you let Nick Testa bat?

(Laughs) I probably never thought about it. I wonder whatever happened to him?

The Giants were playing the Cardinals and in the eleventh or twelfth inning both of your catchers had been taken out. I think you'd run for (Bob) Schmidt and batted for (Valmy) Thomas and you put Testa in and he caught the last inning.

Is that right?

Yeah. That was his only game. I think he would have been the fourth batter up the next inning and you were out of pinch hitters.

So he was going to have to hit. (Laughs)

Yeah. I don't remember who won the game, but it was over and that inning never even started.

I haven't asked you about one of the more famous fellows you played with and managed, but I figured we'd get to him. Who was the best player you ever saw?

The best played I managed was (Willie) Mays, by far. The best player — I don't think there was a tougher competitor than Jackie (Robinson) when he first came up, but I think the best player I had was Mays.

In those early years, when Jackie was carrying the cross of the black man, he carried it with an anger. He played like he was just *mad* at everybody and he played at a pace you'd love your players to play at. He never quit and he never stopped playing and he was a tough guy. Looking back on the quality of the players back in the '50s, he certainly stood out with the best of 'em. There was no doubt about that.

Who was the best pure hitter that you saw?

I thought that (Stan) Musial was. I didn't see (Ted) Williams over in that other league, but I thought Stanley was. It didn't matter left or right or whoever.

I saw Mays when he hit a ton, but it seemed like Musial kind of ground it out all the time. He was *always* there, especially through the '40s and the early '50s. I guess maybe he was the one, of all the hitters, you least liked to see come up with the game on the bases if you were managing or playing against him.

Who was the best pitcher you saw?

I guess (Sandy) Koufax. He was just starting to come into his own when I left the National League and went to the American League, but you could see all the *power* that was there. I never saw Marichal — I was fired (by San Francisco) and two days later they brought Marichal up, which I resented more than the firing. (Laughs) But I thought Sandy was probably the best.

In the American League I got the chance to see Whitey Ford, who was slicker, but for just sheer pitching ability, I'd have to go with Koufax.

Was there a pitcher in your playing days who was particularly tough on you or one you found particularly easy?

Oh, no! None of them were very easy! (Laughs) But Ewell Blackwell could ruin your whole week! I thought he was probably the toughest right-handed pitcher, not only for me but for a lot of right-handed hitters, in the National League. It was just hard to pick him up and he had marvelous stuff. He just didn't last long enough. Blackie was hard and being a sidearmer, something was going to have to give a little bit. He was a little mean and he wasn't against pitching inside — *bad* inside. You had our work to do when you went up against Blackie. (Laughs) He was six-foot-five or six and his control was good enough so he could go at you anywhere he wanted it. I guess Willard Marshall was one of the few who handled him fairly well.

Is there a game that you recall that you did particularly well in?

Yeah, there is. It was April the eighteenth, 1947. The reason I remember it so well is because I've still got the clipping. It was called "This Day in Sports."

On that day Jackie Robinson hit his first major league home run. We were playing the Dodgers and we beat 'em 10-to-6, and I drove in six runs. I hit a grand slam and I hit a two-run home run, so I do remember that.

You managed a long time. You won the 1970 American League West with the Twins. Was that the best team you had?

I think that was the best team because it was the most experienced team.

A team that I thought was going to be the best team was the '59 Giants. Or the '60 Giants. I just didn't stay around long enough to see what they were going to do.

The '59 Giant club was a young club—(Jim) Davenport, Cepeda, even (Willie) McCovey. They were young, but it was an awful good club and I thought we should have won. Maybe if I'd have managed a little better we might have won that year.

In '60, it was much the same club but we had added a few pitching additions in Billy Loes and the little left-hander we got from Baltimore, (Billy) O'Dell, but we didn't lap the field by June so I left there and the club didn't do well. And (Jack) Sanford was on that club. I thought that was a good club.

But the '59 club I thought, up till then, was the best Giant club I'd ever managed.

The most *enjoyable* year I ever had was the '62 Angels.

In '60, the Giants were right there when they let you go.

We were two-and-a-half back. Milwaukee was a good club, Pittsburgh was a good club that year, and we got off a little slow. We were quite a few games over .500, but I guess they felt if the Russians didn't attack we should win it by 20. (Laughs)

You mentioned the '62 Angels. My next question was which team do you feel you did the best job managing. Was that it?

I think so. I learned more about managing that year than I'd ever learned before and I learned about handling pitchers that year. The equation was right and the thinking that I came up with was right.

I wondered why all those players would be available. Evidently people made them available because they didn't think they were top quality. They were all major leaguers but their pitching records were all losing records. You know, guys were seven and twelve, five and ten. I came to the conclusion that maybe someone let them do something that they couldn't do.

We made a couple of deals and got a good staff and I just made up my mind I was going to go with five starters and five short men and there'd be no middle men. The middle man, to me, had no identity and I thought these guys ought to have some identity and we went that way. We used a lot of pitchers but we won 86 games. We led the league on the Fourth of July by not letting guys do things that they weren't capable of doing and letting someone else do it.

We beat Washington two on the Fourth and went ahead of New York, but the *best* series of all was when we went into New York on Labor Day and we had a four-game series there and we split the four with the Yankees.

Then we left there and went and swept Baltimore and came back to Minnesota and Chance tried to pitch a no-hitter and we beat Minnesota, but the Yankees weren't losing anything then, either. We were like two-and-a-half games behind the Yankees and then we came back to earth and the balloon kind of burst. The air came out of us after such a marvelous road trip and we finished third.

The team had some characters. When you have Art Fowler and Ryne Duren, you have some characters but they certainly had some character, too.

A kind of interesting stat on that team: Albie Pearson played center field, I think he played 160 games; Lee Thomas played first base and I think he played 160; and Leon Wagner played 160; and the second baseman, Billy Moran, played 160. Our catcher, Bob Rodgers, caught 155 games. They wanted to play every day. It was fun to watch 'em play and they all executed well, they advanced runners, they did everything well. It was probably the most enjoyable year I ever had.

When everything you do turns out right, you look like a genius. I remember, we were playing against Baltimore and Paul Richards came out to the ballgame — he was going to take over the new Houston franchise — and (Dave) McNally was pitching against us. I had a big pitcher named Don Lee and he was beating 'em two-to-nothing in the seventh inning and I just didn't like him anymore. We got two men on and he was going up to hit. I called him back — he had allowed about three or four hits and he had a good shutout — but there was something I just didn't like.

Richards had said, "I hear you're a genius so I've come out here to watch you." So I put Earl Averill up to pinch hit and he hit a three-run home run and Chance came in and struck out four of the six hitters that were left. When Richards came in, he said, "Well, you've convinced me." (Laughs)

The club responded well, they listened well, the bullpen was great. I think it was one of the few times I had a pitcher that pitched more games than innings — that was Jack Spring. I used him to get a left-hander out and he got just *every* one of them.

You've done everything in baseball at one time or another: you played, you managed, you scouted, you announced, you've been an executive. You've spent your life in baseball. What aspect has been the most satisfying?

Well, I think the most satisfying was too see the development of the young player. To see the Jim Davenports, the Willie McCoveys, to be on the same club and watching Willie Mays develop into such a marvelous player, and then to leave the Giants and watch the Bob Rodgers and Jim Fregosis and Dean Chances come along and see them take their places. Then in later years to come and join this Oakland A's organization and, again, to see the fine players. I think my later years in this business have really been enjoyable because I've had a real chance to be part of building an organization. I've been associated with the Haas family and Sandy Alderson and I think that seeing this all develop and being a part of it — I think that's so satisfying. And to see the players progress and become the players that you hope that they can be.

I guess the other thing is to see some of the players that I've managed go on to be managers — Chuck Tanner and Jimmy Fregosi and now Buck Rodgers. You kind of look back and say, "Maybe somewhere along the line I helped." These are the kind of people you *hoped* would remain in the game. And also Bobby Knoop, who's only been a coach all these years. I always had a feeling that baseball *needed* these kind of people to stay in the game.

When I look around today, I keep looking for those kind of people. Who are the people who are going to stay in and be the managers and be the coaches? It's harder to pick these people because they're all so wealthy and they may not want to hang around.

But that's the satisfaction that you get when you see the development and you get when you have a chance to see them again years later at some of these old-timers' games and it's kind of nice to remember.

I remember the Angels club in '62 and after I left there and managed the Twins and then years later they had some kind of a reunion and I went back. A bunch of them were there and every one of them said it was the best year they could ever remember that they had in baseball. Those are the satisfactions.

But I think the main thing is to watch the young player come in and to watch a team develop into a team like these Oakland A's have.

You mentioned Bobby Knoop. I was always amazed at his range. Did he have the best range of any second baseman?

I don't know if he did. I think (Mike) Gallego probably has the best range of anybody I've seen, but Bobby Knoop made the double play as good as anybody. There were years there when Bobby hit eighth yet drove in a lot of runs and that's an awful tough spot to hit, before the DH, because you don't get an awful lot of good pitches to hit with the pitcher coming up behind you.

I think I would rank him as one of the really *solid* second basemen that I ever saw.

Did you save souvenirs through your career?

Oh, not really. I saved a few, sure. I've got a den that's got a lot of great pictures, but there was nothing like the first hit or anything like that. I've got a ball from every club I've managed and there's enough I'm sure the kids will want some day.

Speaking of kids, your son, Bill, Jr., was minor league executive of the year several years back.

Yeah, right. At Midland (Texas League).

Is he still in baseball?

No, he's in the oil business in Midland. He loved it (baseball) and he did such a good job, but it looked like that was about as far as he was going so he made a choice and now he's doing fine.

Do you get much fan mail?

Oh, yeah. I get, oh, probably an average of 20 letters a week, I would say.

Autograph requests mostly?

Yeah.

And you sign?

Oh, sure.

What do you think of charging for autographs?

I've never done it. I went to one card show. I said, "I'll come if you give the money to Young Life," which is a non-denominational group that deals with teenagers here in the valley. I have a golf tournament and they're the recipient of our charity. They did, so I went and signed some pictures.

I can't sit in judgment on anyone that wants to do that. I guess what bothers me is the answer that's given. It's like the high contracts. They say, "If they want to pay I'm going to take it." I don't know if that justifies it or not. I guess it does but I read where these players say, "If they're willing to pay $25 for my autograph, why shouldn't I take it?" I can't sit in judgment and say they're wrong and I can't say that the system is wrong because evidently someone out there can afford it.

I remember (Jose) Canseco did a real solid thing one spring. The kids were asking him for his autograph — you know, there in Arizona they sit right alongside the entry there when you come out of the clubhouse — and he said no, yet he was going to a card show later where they were going to have to pay 15 bucks or something. It didn't seem like it was a very good balance there, and I think finally somebody got to him and he said, "I'll tell you what I'm going to do. Twice in a week, in the parking lot, after the workouts, I'll sign all autographs." And he did.

It's tough to do it for everybody and a player doesn't like to do it before a game. Players are different now about this. They make so much money that they want to make it forever and they want to get ready to play. And they don't want to be bothered afterwards. I never thought it was too much of a bother. Maybe it was different then, I don't know.

What have been the major changes affecting the game since you began?

I think the main one has been the DH, I would probably say, adding that extra hitter into the American League lineups.

The other one, I think the pitching has changed a lot. Pitching inside is a war now. It was just part of the game 30 years ago — everybody did it, so it was no big deal.

I think those are the two main things. I think the players are the same. There are some marvelous players playing today — I don't think that changes. You know, the Mattinglys and the Boggs' and the Lansfords and Cansecos and those fine players keep coming into the game. Rickey Henderson. So I don't think the *player* changes too much, but I think sometimes the *game* changes.

I think the home run is a bigger item now — except for that Giant club and the Cincinnati club and the Yankee club that all featured that.

Our club is built a lot around the power. And then when you add a fine defense and a good pitching staff, there's not too many things you can't do. And when we added Rickey, we added one more facet — you can walk and be on third in two pitches and win a game.

I think the DH was a big in-road on baseball. I don't think baseball has suffered from it. I don't know if the game's any better with the DH in there. The National League certainly doesn't think that it is. I don't think they'll ever have the DH in the National League, which is fine because then you've got people talking baseball all the time, over whether it's (the DH) good or bad. The fan in the National League doesn't like it and the fan in the American League seems to.

More people are going to baseball now, so evidently we're doing something right at the top of the heap.

Would you do it all again?

Oh, yeah. I wanted to do it when I was nine, so I sure would. There was one regret. I had a chance to manage Detroit back in the '60s and I should have taken it and I didn't. I felt some loyalty to Gene Autry and Bob Reynolds and I stayed there (with the Angels). That would be my only regret because that (Detroit) was a marvelous organization and some wonderful people owned it and ran it and it was a fine team. As a matter of fact, they finally won it in '68 and should have won it in '67.

I don't think I'd change too much more. There's too many good things involved in this lifestyle of ours that you wouldn't want to trade for a nine-to-five, I know that.

* * *

Bill Rigney mentioned the satisfaction of seeing players he managed going on to become managers themselves. Here's the list:

Joe Adcock
Felipe Alou
Joe Amalfitano
Ken Aspromonte
Chuck Cottier
Alvin Dark
Jim Davenport

Jim Fregosi
Whitey Lockman
Frank Quilici
Bob (Buck) Rodgers
Red Schoendienst
Chuck Tanner
Wes Westrum

And here's two who went even farther:

Lee Thomas — Phillies general manager
Bill White — NL president

WILLIAM JOSEPH (SPECS, THE CRICKET) RIGNEY
Born January 29, 1918, Alameda, CA
Ht. 6'1" Wt. 178 Batted and Threw Right

Year	Team	G	AB	R	H	2B	3B	HR	RBI	SB	BA	SA
1946	NYN	110	360	38	85	9	1	3	31	9	.236	.292
1947		130	531	84	142	24	3	17	59	7	.267	.420
1948		113	424	72	112	17	3	10	43	4	.264	.389
1949		122	389	53	108	19	6	6	47	3	.278	.404
1950		56	83	8	15	2	0	0	8	0	.181	.205
1951		44	69	9	16	2	0	4	9	0	.232	.435
1952		60	90	15	27	5	1	1	14	2	.300	.411
1953		19	20	2	5	0	0	0	1	0	.250	.250
8 years		654	1966	281	510	78	14	41	212	25	.259	.376

World Series

Year	Team	G	AB	R	H	2B	3B	HR	RBI	SB	BA	SA
1951	NYN	4	1	1	1	0	0	0	1	0	.250	.250

All-Star Game

Year	League	G	AB	R	H	2B	3B	HR	RBI	SB	BA	SA
1948	National	1	0	0	0	0	0	0	0	0	-	-

CONNIE RYAN

Connie Ryan as Rangers coach (author's photograph).

A Brave in Three Cities
NL All-Star 1944

"When I was younger, I really had a burning desire (to manage)."

— Connie Ryan

Today there are only a few independent minor league teams and all are in Class A. In not too long a time, these will probably be swallowed up just as all the great independent minor league teams of the past have been.

One of the best of these was the Atlanta Crackers of the Southern Association, which signed, developed, and sold many, many future major league stars. Owned by Atlanta at one time or another on the way up were such players as Billy Goodman, Luke Appling, Davey Williams, Taffy Wright (an absolute hitting machine — look him up), Hugh Casey, Ed Wright, Kirby Higbe, Connie Ryan, etc.

Many — most — of these guys didn't start out with the Crackers. Like the Major League clubs, Atlanta sent its players out to other, lower classifications until they were ready to play in Atlanta.

Connie Ryan, for instance, spent his first professional season — 1940 — playing for Savannah in the South Atlantic League, where he batted .316 and showed good punch for a second baseman (13 HR, 73 RBI). He had been signed off the LSU campus, even then a proving ground for future major league talent.

Connie moved to Atlanta in 1941 and batted an even .300 with 83 RBIs. At the end of that season, the New York Giants bought him and he spent most of '42 with Jersey City (International League).

On April 27, 1943, he and catcher Hugh Poland were traded to the Boston Braves. Boston had lost its second baseman, Sibby Sisti, to the war effort, and must have thought highly of Ryan because 1942's NL batting champ, Ernie Lombardi, was sent to New York in exchange.

Connie struggled in '43 as the Braves' everyday second sacker, batting only .212 (one point better than Sisti had managed in '42). But in 1944 he was the NL's best at the position, a fact acknowledged when he was chosen as the starter for the All-Star Game.

And he had a great game. The NL hadn't won since 1940 but on that July 11 they downed the AL, 7–1. Connie played the whole game, went 2-for-4, scored a run, stole the only base of the game, and set a new All-Star Game record for chances by a second baseman (nine, breaking Frankie Frisch's record of eight set back in the first game in 1933 — the record has since been equalled twice, by Bill Mazeroski in 1958 and by Juan Samuel in 1987).

Like Sisti, World War II got Connie. Right after the All-Star Game the Navy took him. He returned in '46 and remained in the majors until early 1954. He spent the rest of that season with Louisville (American Association) and then was playing manager for Corpus Christi (Big State League) and Austin (Texas League) in 1955 and '56.

He is one of two men to be in uniform in all three cities the Braves have called home. (The other is Eddie Mathews.) He was a player in Boston, a coach in Milwaukee, and a coach and manager in Atlanta. And he is one of two men to be in uniform for the Braves in both the '48 and '57 World Series. (The other is Warren Spahn.)

On April 14, 1953, while playing for the Phillies against the Pirates in Pittsburgh, Connie went 6-for-6 in a nine-inning game, but the Pirates won it, 14–12. Six or more hits in a game is getting less frequent. Only twice in the decade of the 1950s did a National Leaguer accomplish it. Breaking down major league baseball into three "eras," we see how much this feat is diminishing:

ERA	YEARS	6-Hit Games	Frequency
1876–1900	25	53	approx. 2/year
1901–1940	40	41	approx. 1/year
1941–1992	52	29	approx. ½ year

Connie stayed in baseball after retiring as a player, but now he's back home after over a half century in the game.

The Atlanta Crackers signed you in 1940.

Connie Ryan: The Crackers were independently owned. I think Coca-Cola owned it and Earl Mann bought it from Coca-Cola. I was owned by the Giants in '42 and into '43. I was traded early (in '43) to Boston.

In your second year, you were voted to the All-Star team.

That was pretty exciting. I thoroughly enjoyed it. It was a memorable time.

Then Uncle Sam got you.

Right after the All-Star Game. I was drafted.

I went up to Finger Lakes, N.Y., for indoctrination, supposedly for 12 to 20 weeks or so. Something came up and they formed a team of baseball players and they sent 'em over to Pearl Harbor, so I went along with that group — we were all major league players — and then eventually they sent us out to play exhibition games on Tinian, Saipan, and all those islands.

To make a long story short, Admiral Nimitz said, "Leave 'em out there and disperse 'em to various islands." I wound up on Guam.

We continued to play ball, but (the fields) were like concrete. We had to take care of the recreation area for the ships that docked there and and we played against some of the ships.

I came back (after the war) and I started off well. I think it was in June I sprained my ankle and played on it, which I never should have done, and it just set me back in everything. I lost my batting stroke and everything and that was a wasted year.

In a 1949 game, you went to the on-deck circle wearing a raincoat.

Connie Ryan (courtesy of *The National Pastime*).

 We were playing the Brooklyn Dodgers and it was a double-header late in the season in September (the 29th) in Boston. It was a very misty and cold day and we had an off-day the next day — both teams. The umpire wouldn't call it, so I borrowed the groundskeeper's nor'wester and put it on and went up to hit, but I didn't get up to the plate. George Barr was the umpire and he threw me out of the game. There wasn't many people in the stands to see that.

You were traded to Cincinnati in 1950. What did you think of leaving the Braves?

I never gave it a thought 'cause I had nowhere to go with the Braves at the time and it was a breath of fresh air. I enjoyed my stay at Cincinnati. I stayed there two years and was traded to Philadelphia and I enjoyed Philadelphia, too.

You probably had your best overall years with those two teams from 1950 through 1952.

I don't know what happened in '53. I was hitting real good. I think I would have hit close to .300 or over that year, but (manager) Steve O'Neill decided to bring up a young player that we had given a lot of money to and all of a sudden I was sitting down.

Ted Kazanski?

Right. I wasn't playing too good in the field. Maybe that had something to do with it.

Willie Jones was playing third base at the time. I could never understand why O'Neill didn't move me over to third base for a week to see how it went because Jones was hitting about .220.

You went 6-for-6 in a game in 1953.

That was a record for a while until that Pittsburgh player — he was a second baseman, too — (Rennie) Stennett, went 7-for-7 (September 16, 1975).

Do you consider that to be your best game?

Cumulative game, maybe, but I don't know if that was my best game or not. You remember getting some important hits.

I didn't realize what was happening till I was 5-for-5. (Ralph) Kiner was playing first base (for Pittsburgh) that day and he said, "Gee, you're getting a lot of hits." I said, "Yeah, now that you mention it, I think that's five." (Laughs)

What was the most thrilling event in your career?

The day I was traded from the Giants to Boston. Casey Stengel was the manager of Boston and I pinch-hit in the ninth inning in a nothing-to-nothing game and hit a home run and won it, two-to-nothing. (Laughs) That kinda stands out.

Who's the best player you saw?

I think Henry Aaron, day-in and day-out. Henry just went about his business so easy and he never really looked like he was extending himself. I guess he was in his own way, but he never really looked like it. He was a great hitter. He and (Stan) Musial, I guess, were the two best hitters that I've seen.

As a Braves coach, you saw Aaron in both Milwaukee and Atlanta.

I only coached one year, in '57 (in Milwaukee), and then I came back in '72 and stayed a few years with the Braves. I was connected with them a long time. I scouted for 'em.

Who was the best pitcher?

The toughest pitcher was Ewell Blackwell. He was outstanding. I think if he wouldn't have hurt his arm he would have been something. It was life-and-death just to keep yourself in there at the plate. He was the toughest pitcher I ever faced.

(Don) Newcombe always gave me fits, too. Newcombe was a good pitcher.

Talking about great pitchers, you can't overlook the fact that I played with one of the best: (Warren) Spahn. Day-in and day-out, he was probably the finest and most durable pitcher. He was excellent. 363 wins. That's more than a lot of guys get hits. (Laughs)

What about Johnny Sain?

Great. If he threw five fastballs in a ballgame it was funny. Nothing but breaking balls. He was a great competitor.

They said, "Spahn and Sain and pray for rain" in '48, but you guys had other pitchers.

Vern Bickford was a good competitor, also. He was steady. Nelson Potter came over there and filled in.

And (manager Billy) Southworth did a hell of a job in those days. He was well ahead of his time. He had grievance committees for the players and those type of things off the field. He was a good man.

You got the only hit, a two-out eighth-inning single, off of Bucky Walters in a game on May 14, 1944. He was a pretty good pitcher.

Oh, *definitely*!

Should he be in the Hall of Fame?

I would think so. Sure.

You were an interim manager twice — once with Atlanta and once with Texas. Did you ever have the desire to be a manager?

When I was younger, I really had a burning desire. If I'd have got offered the manager's job in Atlanta after being the interim, I would have taken it but I wasn't offered it.

In Texas, they offered me the job and I turned it down. To this day I don't know why. I was a little older then, but that's probably the biggest mistake I ever made.

Did you save souvenirs from your career?

I really wasn't a big saver. I doubt very much that a lot of people were in those days. I've got scrapbooks that various people in my family have saved for me, but as far as mementos, no. It didn't cross your mind.

The memorabilia is worth so much. A friend of mine sold a Babe Ruth bat for $10,000. It was autographed. Those kind of things you gotta sell.

Would you go back and be a baseball player again?

Oh, I think I would. Yes. No question about it. I enjoyed it.

Connie Ryan's two terms as interim manager were short. In 1975 he took over the Braves' helm with about a month to go in the season. After 134 games, Clyde King had them buried in fifth place in the NL West in what was to be the first year of a five-year slide for the team (it finished in the cellar the next four years).

Then in 1977 he guided the Texas Rangers for six games as the third of four managers for the team that year. Frank Lucchesi was fired two months into the season and Eddie Stanky was named to replace him. After one game (a win), Stanky decided he was "homesick" so he quit without warning. Rangers' management was up a creek with no manager, so they quickly named Connie to the position while they regrouped to search for a new pilot. Finally the field was narrowed to Connie and Billy Hunter, then a coach with the Orioles. When Connie declined the job, Hunter accepted it.

CORNELIUS JOSEPH RYAN
Born February 27, 1920, New Orleans, LA
Died January 3, 1996, New Orleans, LA
Ht. 5'11"   Wt. 175   Batted and Threw Right

Year	Team	G	AB	R	H	2B	3B	HR	RBI	SB	BA	SA
1942	NYN	11	27	4	5	0	0	0	2	1	.185	.185
1943	BosN	132	457	52	97	10	2	1	24	7	.212	.249
1944		88	332	56	98	18	5	4	25	13	.295	.416
1946		143	502	55	121	28	8	1	48	7	.241	.335
1947		150	544	60	144	33	5	5	69	5	.265	.371
1948		51	122	14	26	3	0	0	10	0	.213	.238
1949		85	208	28	52	13	1	6	20	1	.250	.409
1950	BosN	20	72	12	14	2	0	3	6	0	.194	.347
	CinN	106	367	45	95	18	5	3	43	4	.259	.360
	Year	126	439	57	109	20	5	6	49	4	.248	.358
1951	CinN	136	473	75	112	17	4	16	53	11	.237	.391
1952	PhiN	154*	577	81	139	24	6	12	49	13	.241	.366
1953	PhiN	90	247	47	73	14	6	5	26	5	.296	.462
	ChiA	17	54	6	12	1	0	0	6	2	.222	.241
	Year	107	301	53	85	15	6	5	32	7	.282	.422
1954	CinN	1	0	0	0	0	0	0	0	0	-	-
12 years		1184	3982	535	988	181	42	56	381	69	.248	.357

*Led league

World Series

Year	Team	G	AB	R	H	2B	3B	HR	RBI	SB	BA	SA
1948	BosA	2	1	0	0	0	0	0	0	0	.000	.000

All-Star Game

Year	League	G	AB	R	H	2B	3B	HR	RBI	SB	BA	SA
1948	National	1	4	1	2	0	0	0	0	1	.500	.500

DICK SISLER

Dick Sisler as Reds manager (courtesy of Cincinnati Reds).

The Whiz Kids' Biggest Hit
NL All-Star 1950

"The earliest I remember ... was when I was out at the ballpark and Babe Ruth or Lou Gehrig stopped by the box to say hello to my mother."

— Dick Sisler

Famous home runs are a favorite topic. When fans discuss them, or when writer's write about them, there are several which are always brought up: Bobby Thomson's "shot heard 'round the world," Babe Ruth's "called shot," Gabby Hartnett's "homer in the gloamin'," Kirk Gibson's World Series blast off Dennis Eckersley, Ted Williams' All-Star Game round-tripper off Rip Sewell, Roger Maris' number 61, Henry Aaron's number 715, Bill Mazeroski's Series' winner.

But come on, guys. There's one every bit as important as any of those and *more* important than most of them. It's *the* most important home run in Philadelphia baseball history—American *or* National League.

The Phillies won a pennant in 1915 and then fell into oblivion. People talk of the inabilities of the Browns and Senators. Today, a lot of ink goes to the woes of the Cubs. But *never, ever* has there been a run of inferiority such as the Phillies experienced from 1918 through 1948. "Bad" is much too gentle a word for the team over that period.

Finally, though, in 1950 the Phillies won their second pennant.

The season had opened well for the Phils. Coming off a third-place finish in 1949 (their highest finish and best record since 1917), manager Eddie Sawyer had several young potential stars who gave the local fans reason for some optimism. "Young," however, was the key word here. No team in the NL fielded a younger starting eight—25.9-years-old—and no team in either league had a younger rotation—the top five starters averaged 23.8 years.

And, as we said, the season began well. They opened at home against the defending NL champion Dodgers. The starters were Robin Roberts for Philadelphia and Don Newcombe for Brooklyn and Roberts came out on top to give the Phils a one-game lead over the Bums. One hundred fifty-two games later, going into the final game of the season, they still had that one game lead, but a lot had happened in between.

On September 20, Philadelphia had widened the gap to 7½ games with only 11 to play. However, they lost six of the next nine (to give a preview of 1964). Meanwhile, Brooklyn, the favorite to repeat, got hot. The Dodgers won 13 of 16 and on September 30 the Phillies' lead was only two games and, in a brilliant if fortunate scheduling arrangement, the two teams met in Brooklyn for two games on the final weekend of the season.

The Phils had to win only one of the two but their pitching staff was in trouble. Three of their top five starters were out. In one of the most ill-timed moves our military ever made, 17-game winner Curt Simmons was called up on September 10. Rookie Bob Miller's arm was bothering him and rookie Bubba Church had been hit in the face by a line drive on September 15. On top of that, catcher Andy Seminick had suffered an ankle injury a few days before in a home plate collision with Monte Irvin of the Giants.

On Saturday, September 30, the lead shrank to one game. Erv Palica, only 22 years old, pitched the Dodgers to a 7–3 victory in an outstanding clutch performance. (Much was expected of Palica but he later fell into disfavor with Brooklyn's front office when Buzzie Bavasi labeled him "gutless." A gutless pitcher does not win a crucial game as Palica did.)

So now the Phils had dropped seven of ten and the stage was set for high drama. Philadelphia's pitching was gone. If the Dodgers won and forced a playoff it would be no contest. Sawyer picked 19-game winner Roberts to start the finale — his third start in five days. Dodger manager Burt Shotton went with his ace, Newcombe, also with 19 wins. It was the same matchup that had begun the season nearly six months before.

(Newcombe had given one of the year's top performances a few weeks earlier. On September 6, he shut out the Phillies 2–0, in the first game of a double-header and then came back to hurl seven innings in the nightcap but left for a pinch-hitter, trailing 2–0.)

Philadelphia scored first but Pee Wee Reese homered in the sixth to tie it at 1–1. Reese's homer was one of the biggest flukes in the history of the game. The ball landed on a ledge in right field and stayed there, in play but unreachable, as Pee Wee rounded the bases. (The next season, the ledge was ruled a ground-rule double.)

The score stayed that way until the bottom of the ninth. Roberts walked Cal Abrams to begin the inning and Reese lined a single to left. Duke Snider was up next with Jackie Robinson to follow. Everyone was expecting Duke to bunt but he swung away and lined a bullet to the right of second base. The first thought was that second baseman Mike Goliat would catch it but it went by him. Abrams, though, couldn't break until he saw it go by Goliat.

Center fielder Richie Ashburn had been expecting a bunt, also, and had been creeping in in case he needed to back up a play at second, so when Snider's hit got through the infield Ashburn was already farther in than normal. Abrams was sent home by the third base coach because of Ashburn's weak arm, but Richie got the ball on one hop and came up throwing. Abrams was out at home by 15 or 20 feet.

With one out, Roberts then walked Robinson intentionally to load the bases and got Carl Furillo to pop up and Gil Hodges to fly harmlessly to Del Ennis, who momentarily lost the ball in the sun, in right.

In the top of the tenth, Roberts, a good-hitting pitcher, led off with a single up the middle. Then Eddie Waitkus blooped a single to right-center. With runners on first and second, Ashburn tried to sacrifice but Roberts was thrown out at third.

With one out and runners on first and second, left fielder Dick Sisler came up. Sisler was second on the team in batting and third in RBIs and had played in the All-Star Game that year, but, more importantly, he had already gotten three hits off Newk that day. He blasted a long drive into the left field seats, making the score 4–1.

Dick Sisler (courtesy of *The National Pastime*).

That took all the fire out of the Dodgers. Roberts set them down in order in the bottom of the tenth and the Phillies — the Whiz Kids — had a pennant for the City of Brotherly Love, their first NL flag in 35 years.

So why isn't this home run mentioned when the great home runs are spoken of? An extra-inning shot off a great pitcher on the last day of a season to win a pennant. It sure sounds pretty great.

Maybe if there had been two outs. Or maybe if it had been hit in the *bottom* of the inning. Certainly if it had been hit by a New York player — take your pick — Yankees, Giants, or Dodgers. Maybe if one of these scenarios had occurred people would talk about it today more than they do.

(The Dodgers and Phillies closed out three consecutive seasons with extra-inning games and all three were crucial. In 1949, Brooklyn had to beat Philadelphia in ten to hold off St. Louis and in 1951 the Dodgers had to get by the Phils in 14 in order to force the playoff—and set up Thomson's home run—with the Giants.)

Dick Sisler did a whole lot more than hit this home run. He was born to baseball—his father was Hall of Famer George Sisler, little brother Dave pitched eight years in the major leagues, and big brother George, Jr., had a long career as a baseball executive.

Dick left the majors during the 1953 season but played in the minors through 1958. He managed for four years in the minors beginning in '57 and in '61 joined the Cincinnati Reds as a coach. When Fred Hutchinson's health prevented him from continuing as the Reds manager, Dick took over. He guided the team for the final third of 1964 and all of 1965 and did a great job.

The team he inherited from Hutch was in third place and the Phillies seemed to be on their way to their first pennant since 1950, but this was the year of the Fizz Kids and as the Phils folded the Cardinals, Reds, Giants, and Braves all closed with a rush.

On October 4, the final day of the season, Sisler had rallied his squad to a tie for first with the Cardinals and the Phillies had dropped one behind. The schedule favored St. Louis, however—they were playing the Mets, in tenth, 13 games behind ninth place Houston—while Cincinnati had to play Philadelphia. Wins that day by the Phillies and Mets would have meant a three-way tie for first, and Philadelphia did win but St. Louis downed New York to win by a game over both Cincy and Philadelphia with San Francisco only three back and Milwaukee but five behind. It was the Cardinals' first flag in 18 years.

In 1965, Dick's last season as Reds' manager, there were high hopes for the team but they faded to fourth, although still 16 games over .500. Dick was not rehired for '66, a year which saw Cincinnati drop to seventh and below .500 without him. In his year-and-a-third of big league managing, his record was 121-94 (.563)—that compares favorably with anyone. Look it up.

Dick Sisler spent several more years as a batting coach. He's been retired for over a decade now.

You were born to baseball.

Dick Sisler: That's right. I was in a baseball family. My father was one of the greats and I just happened to have the ability to play in high school and also in college and then I went into the minor leagues and I graduated up to the majors.

You were around baseball from Day One. What's your earliest memory of the game?

Oh, for goodness sakes, yes. The earliest I remember—this might sound phony—was when I was out at the ballpark and my dad, of course, was a great ballplayer and Babe Ruth or Lou Gehrig stopped by the box over there to say hello to my mother. That's the earliest I can remember and that's a long time ago.

Did you hang around the ballpark with your father as you were growing up?

No, not much, because I had to go to school. But then during the summer, oh, yes — I've been in a whole lot of clubhouses and I've been told to get out of clubhouses when I was a little boy. (Laughs) I was around it a lot.

You signed your first contract at age 18.

I went to Colgate University for about a year, then I dropped out of there and I went into baseball.

If I can remember right, I went down to Cuba and I had a whale of a year down there. I broke all their home run records, then I came up with the Cardinals. That was in 1946.

You got into the World Series as a rookie.

Yeah, I was lucky. Yes, sir. A whole lot of guys don't ever get into it. That was my first year and I was in there and that was a real thrill.

You were traded to the Phillies in 1948 for Ralph LaPointe and $20,000. What did you think of that?

I didn't like it at first, but the way it turned out it was the biggest break I ever had. You know, you hate to leave a ballclub — you know all the guys and you have to go to a new one and make new friends and everything.

The Phillies sure got the better end of the deal. LaPointe had looked pretty good as a rookie in 1947 but did nothing after he was traded.

Yeah, he didn't do anything at all.

With the Phillies, you were a regular either at first base or in the outfield for four years. You made the All-Star team in 1950. I bet that was exciting.

That was. That was a real thrill, one of the biggest ones I've ever had. I pinch-hit (for Newcombe). I got 1-for-1.

That was the only hit Bob Lemon gave up in his three innings.

That's right. I was lucky. He gave me a good pitch to hit and I singled to right. (Pee Wee Reese then ran for Dick.)

On October 1, 1950, you had probably the biggest hit in the history of the Phillies.

Yes, I guess it was because it was a pennant-winning home run.

I've had a whole lot of thrills in baseball. You always have those playing against the guys that you used to read about. I cherish all those memories.

What is the biggest thrill you had?

It would be that home run, I guess.

Newcombe figured in both of your biggest moments, didn't he?

(Laughs) I was lucky. And then I had some good years managing and coaching. I had just a real fine career.

What do you remember about Ashburn's throw?

Ashburn actually did not have a good arm and I think it surprised everyone when he threw out Abrams. 'Course, the ball was in short center. I mean, it wasn't a real long throw but it turned out to be a very important throw. And it surprised everyone.

What about Jim Konstanty that year?

What a year he had. The thing is, you had to bat against a Roberts and a Simmons and then Konstanty came in there with all that junk. It kind of threw off all the hitters.

Some people have said that Simmons could probably throw harder than Roberts at that point. Is that true?

One was right-handed, the other was left-handed. I think Roberts had the ideal control, had the better control of the two. Later on I had to bat against 'em, after I was traded away from there. I got to know both of 'em and they were both great. (Laughs)

In the 1950 World Series, the Yankee pitchers just absolutely shut you guys down.

I think it was actually anti-climactic. We didn't win it till the last day. Of course, I'm not taking anything away from the Yankees, either, because they had some great pitchers, too.

They pitched me in so tight, you know. I believe I only got one hit. That was off either (Eddie) Lopat or (Whitey) Ford. They had a real good ballclub.

And they had had time to arrange their rotation. That's a big advantage.

Oh, absolutely.

Your first managerial post was at Nashville in 1957. Were you trying to become a manager?

I thought I would try it out, you know. When I first started out I was a playing manager. Nashville had that short right field wall, but that didn't have anything to do with my decision. I just thought I would go into the business end of it, to the managing end of it.

After a few years of minor league managing and coaching for the Reds, you became Cincinnati's manager in 1964. Your record with the Reds was outstanding in the short period you were there. Did you want to keep managing?

Oh, yeah. It wasn't up to me. It was up to Bill DeWitt.

Were there other opportunities?

I didn't go after them sincerely. I put my name in the pot a few times, but that was about it.

You coached for several years, up until about ten years ago.

I liked coaching. I was a batting coach and I liked to coach that because I've talked to all the great hitters: Williams and, of course, my dad and Dimaggio and all of 'em. I've taught their theories on hitting, you know. Then I proceeded to go on my own. I had some good years that way.

Speaking of batting, who was the best hitter that you saw?

Oh, I think (Ted) Williams. I think for downright just hitting it would be Williams, and I guess all the way around it would be (Joe) DiMaggio.

DiMaggio over Willie Mays?

Yeah, I would say so. I would think DiMaggio was perhaps a little bit better all the way around, in my opinion. Of course, after all, they're both great.

Who was the best pitcher?

I'd say (Bob) Feller. I batted against him while I was in the Navy and, boy, he really had *outstanding* stuff— outstanding fastball, outstanding curveball, it would drop off a table. I think he's the only one that ever struck me out three times in a game. Three out of four times and the one time I hit the ball I was so pleased about it I didn't know what to do. (Laughs)

I think he got a lot of guys three times.

Yeah, I think so, too. A lot perhaps four times.

Do you get much fan mail today?

I don't count it but I get some almost every day.

The Sisler name is a huge one and with you hitting one of the important home runs, I would think that you are probably well sought-after.

Yes. I get a lot of invitations and I get a lot of fan mail. Most of it's autograph requests. I sign 'em all.

Did you save souvenirs from your career or your dad's career?

No, not much. I gave some to some real close friends of mine and also my children. I gave them balls and bats and so on.

Did any of your children play ball?

My boy tried but they told him they didn't ever think that he would get to the major leagues as a player, so he's in the business end of baseball now. He works for the Cardinals in the minor leagues.

Any regrets?

Oh, you always have some regrets but they're not real serious because when you've had luck and you've had the good Lord behind you that you didn't get hurt, that all adds into it.

I was real pleased with my career. I enjoyed every minute of it.

Would you go back and do it all again?

I sure would.

* * *

The 1950 season was Dick Sisler's most memorable: All-Star Game, pennant-winning home run, World Series, and one more highlight. He had eight consecutive hits that year. Teammate Eddie Waitkus also had eight in a row at one point that season. That's the only time teammates had ever accomplished that in the same year.

RICHARD ALLAN SISLER
Born November 2, 1920, St. Louis, MO
Ht. 6'2"   Wt. 205   Batted Left   Threw Right

Year	Team	G	AB	R	H	2B	3B	HR	RBI	SB	BA	SA
1946	StLN	83	235	17	61	11	2	3	42	0	.260	.362
1947		46	74	4	15	2	1	0	9	0	.203	.257
1948	PhiN	121	446	60	122	21	3	11	56	1	.274	.408
1949		121	412	42	119	19	6	7	50	0	.289	.415
1950		141	523	79	155	29	4	13	83	1	.296	.442
1951		125	428	46	123	20	5	8	52	1	.287	.414
1952	CinN	11	27	3	5	1	1	0	4	0	.185	.296
	StLN	119	418	48	109	14	5	13	60	3	.261	.411
	Year	130	445	51	114	15	6	13	64	3	.256	.404
1953	StLN	32	43	3	11	1	1	0	4	0	.256	.326
8 years		799	2606	302	720	118	28	55	360	6	.276	.406

World Series

Year	Team	G	AB	R	H	2B	3B	HR	RBI	SB	BA	SA
1946	StLN	2	2	0	0	0	0	0	0	0	.000	.000
1950	PhiN	4	17	0	1	0	0	0	1	0	.059	.059
2 years		6	19	0	1	0	0	0	1	0	.053	.053

All-Star Game

Year	League	G	AB	R	H	2B	3B	HR	RBI	SB	BA	SA
1950	National	1	1	0	1	0	0	0	0	0	1.000	1.000

BILL VOISELLE

Bill Voiselle (George Brace photograph).

No. 96
NL All-Star 1944

"It hurts 'em every time they expand. They don't have enough pitchers to go around..."

— Bill Voiselle

"Spahn and Sain and two days of rain." Catchy phrase. One of the most famous in baseball history.

But not very accurate.

Spahn and Sain had plenty of help. Good help. Here's the top performers from the 1948 Boston Braves' pitching staff:

	W-L	ERA
Johnny Sain	24-15	2.60
Warren Spahn	15-12	3.71
BILL VOISELLE	13-13	3.63
Vern Bickford	11-5	3.27
Bobby Hogue	8-2	3.24
Red Barrett	7-8	3.66
Clyde Shoun	5-1	4.01
Nelson Potter	5-2	2.33

The World Series of 1948 marked Boston's first National League appearance since the 1914 Miracle Braves. The American League representatives in '48 were the Cleveland Indians, that team's first post-season action since 1920. The two teams' total of 62 consecutive years is the longest combined championship drought ever.

The Braves won their league with a revamped lineup, not a two-man pitching staff. In fact, in '47, Spahn and Sain had more wins than they did in '48 (42 to 39), yet the team finished third, eight games behind the Dodgers.

Four rookies played significant roles in bringing Boston to the top: Rookie-of-the-Year Alvin Dark was the shortstop, Clint Conatser was platooned in the outfield, and Bickford and Hogue accounted for 19 wins.

And to balance this infusion of youth, several veterans were acquired. Bill Voiselle was the first, joining the club in mid–'47 from the Giants. Then Jeff Heath was purchased from the Browns (always in need of cash) in December. Eddie Stanky came from the Dodgers in a spring training, '48, trade. And, finally, Nelson Potter was purchased from the Philadelphia Athletics in June of '48.

These players, added to the nucleus of talent already there, enabled manager Billy Southworth to lead his Braves to the top of the NL.

As quickly as it came, however, it went. In '49, injuries and trades brought the team back into the pack. But for one year, the Boston Braves were darned near the best team in baseball.

Bill Voiselle, who wore number 96 in honor of his hometown of Ninety Six, South Carolina, was a key member of the '48 squad.

In 1944 — your official rookie year — you had an overpowering season.

Bill Voiselle: I should've won 30 that year. (Laughs) I'm not braggin', but I lost six in a row and my earned run average was oh-eight-nine for the six games. The Giants didn't have much that year.

You were selected for the All-Star Game. How many wins did you have at that point?

I think I'd done won nine or ten.

You had come up with the Giants at the ends of both 1942 and '43. What kind of minor league record had you had?

I don't remember. All I remember is the Giants had a working agreement with Oklahoma City and they took me at the end of the season, 1942. I think I pitched one game.

Then they sent me to Jersey City in '43 and brought me back up at the end of the season.

Is it true that Giants manager Mel Ott once fined you $500 for letting a man hit an 0-2 pitch?

That was the next year. After I'd done pitched 313 innin's and I had 28 complete games the year before, I was 9-and-0 that year in '45. I hadn't lost a ballgame and we got to St. Louis and I had 'em 2-to-1 in the ninth. Two outs in the ninth innin' and I got two strikes on Johnny Hopp and I tried to waste it — I threw it over his head and he reached up and hit it for a triple.

Then it came up a storm! I mean, it liked to blowed the lights down! I had to go in the dugout. I sit there for 45 minutes and Ott was mad 'cause I let him hit the 0-2 pitch so he put me back in after I set there all that time. I think Ray Sanders got a hit and tied it up and then somebody else hit one. It took a bad hop over my outfielder's head and I got beat, 3-to-2.

I come in and he (Ott) said, "I'm not gonna fine you a hundred. I'm gonna fine you *five* hundred and I oughta make it a thousand!" If I'd a said anything, he'd have probably fined me that thousand.

How much were you making that year?

(Laughs) Ten thousand. That's all you could make back in them days.

Is it true that another time you threw an 0-2 pitch that the umpire called a strike and you argued with him that it wasn't?

That wasn't me, but it was somebody on the Giants. Ott said any time anybody let a batter hit a 0-2 pitch, it'd be a hundred dollars. That one guy throwed it and the umpire called it a strike and he hollered, "Aw, that wasn't a strike!" (Laughs) I forget who that was.

You went to the Boston Braves in '47 and in '48 you guys went to the World Series. The slogan was "Spahn and Sain and two days of rain," but that was not a two-man pitching staff.

Oh yeah. Bickford and Hogue and Red Barrett. I won 13 and all them others did a good job. Ol' Nelson Potter pitched good ball for us that year. It was no two-man pitching staff—they tried to make out like it was.

See, Spahn didn't come into his own till later. He was just a little ol' boy. I roomed with Warren for about three years.

The World Series that year—you pitched real well in relief and then started the last game and pitched well there, too.

I remember goin' in that third game. I think the bases was loaded and one out and I got 'em out. They didn't score the rest of the ballgame. I think we was behind two-to-nothin' when I went in and that's the way the game ended up. Me and Red Barrett, we held 'em the rest of the way.

I believe that's the day we had 80,000. That was the biggest crowd they ever had at a World Series. They had 15,000 people standin' in the outfield—they roped it off. Any kind of a fly ball was a home run because of all the people standin' around out there. Standin' room only. That's why so many home runs was hit a couple of games later. So many people wanted to see, they just roped off the outfield and let 'em in.

I had never been beaten by the American League in spring training and these city series until Game Six, when it really counted. (Laughs) In about the fifth or sixth innin', I believe it was, we had the bases loaded. We were tied up, 1-to-1, and Southworth let me hit with two outs. (Laughs) That caused a lot of second guessin', you know.

The beginnin' of the next innin', ol' Joe Gordon come up and I hung him a curve and he hit a home run. So they *really* second-guessed Southworth then. (Laughs)

Clint Conatser pinch-hit for you in the eighth.

Yep. He got a sacrifice fly. You know, we come awful close to tyin' that game up a couple of times there. We had the men on but couldn't get 'em in.

What hurt us a lot was Jeff Heath gettin' his leg broke. He played with Cleveland all them many years and he was our home run hitter. The last game we played in Brooklyn he slid in home and he just turned that foot right around. He didn't get to play.

In '49 you won seven games and four were shutouts.

Yep. I didn't get to pitch too much that year. He'd tell me, "Do your runnin' and go on home. You're pitchin' tomorrow." Well, I'd run, I'd go home. I'd go back out there the next night and he'd say somebody else wanted to pitch. So he told me to do my runnin'. I thought I was on a track team. (Laughs)

You left the majors in 1950 and you were only 31 years old.

They swapped me to the Cubs and the Cubs sent me to Springfield and at the end of the season I didn't want to go back up. I told 'em I'd rather go home than go back to the Cubs.

The next year they traded me and Hank Edwards for Dee Fondy and the

Bill Voiselle (courtesy of *The National Pastime*).

Rifleman, (Chuck) Connors. We went to the Dodgers. In spring training, when it was over, they sent me to Montreal. We won the pennant and got in the Little World Series. Walter Alston was managing Montreal then. Tommy Lasorda was one of the pitchers on that team.

The next year they wanted me to go to St. Paul and I just asked for my release. They give it to me. After I got my release I went back to Richmond. I believe I broke the International League record with Richmond that year. I was in 72 games. I believe that was the record then. I don't know if it's been broken.

When did you retire from baseball?
I believe it was in 1957.

You wore number 96, the highest number ever worn by a major leaguer until Mitch Williams wore number 99 in 1993. Whose idea was that?
It was Boston's. Little ol' Shorty Young up there, he wanted me to wear

number 96. We had to get permission from the commissioner. He said I could wear it.

Is there one game that stands out in your memory?

The one I remember most, I reckon, I was pitchin' against the Cubs. I had 'em one-to-nothin', two outs in the ninth innin'. Billy Jurges, he was the captain of the Giants, and he had played with the Cubs a long, long time. Ol' big Bill Nicholson, a great big ol' left-hand hitter — he was the hitter. The catcher called time. He come out and Billy Jurges says, "Y'all get together. You know what this big guy's gonna try to do." I says, "Yeah, he's gonna try to hit it over that row of houses over yonder." (Laughs) So the catcher says, "Just throw him a slow curve." I said, "Nooo. If I'm gonna throw a curve, I want to throw it just as *hard* as I can and break it right straight down." He said, "Okay, we'll do that."

So we curved him. When he hit that ball, when I looked up, I knew it was gone. (Laughs) My heart, it done sunk. But it happened to be one he got under and it got right out to the fence and ol' (Red) Treadway caught it. I looked out there and threw my chest back out and went walkin' in and beat 'em one-to-nothin'. But when that ball went over my head, I knew it was gone.

He always hit me pretty good, Bill Nicholson.

Who was the best player you saw?

You have to take Stan Musial. But you know, Musial hit everybody. It's always somebody else, like Nicholson. He wore me out. I remember Gene Hermanski. He always hit Sain pretty good.

The good hitters, like Musial and Ted Williams, they hit everybody.

Was Nicholson the toughest on you?

He was the toughest I *ever* pitched to.

Who was the best pitcher?

Bob Feller, Ewell Blackwell, and Johnny Sain in '48.

Blackwell was about six-foot-five and threw sidearm. You didn't even feel good sittin' in the dugout when he pitched. (Laughs)

Was there a team you had either good luck or bad luck with?

I always had real *good* luck against the Dodgers. I had bad luck against Cincinnati. Cincinnati had nine right-handed hitters and I'd sidearm 'em but I think I didn't beat 'em but two times the whole time I was up there. I'd get beat one-to-nothin', 2-to-1.

What's the biggest change in baseball?

Addin' more teams. It hurts 'em every time they expand. They don't have enough pitchers to go around now and they're gettin' two more (teams) in the National League. Sometimes when they want to argue with you, you just say take four teams away from the National League and add (the players) to the eight left and see if it wouldn't be better baseball than what they got now.

Bill Voiselle 169

When we played, they had eight teams in the American League and eight in the National League and they had three good Triple-A leagues and then they come down to Double-A, A, B, C, D.

Back when we played they'd hit .333 — that's just one hit every three times up. These guys today are hittin' .220 — that's about one hit a month.

Do you get much fan mail today?

Yeah. We get right smart. Autographs. I can always tell when I get a write-up or somethin' 'cause here come the autographs. These kids'll say, "I never did see you pitch, but my granddaddy says you could pitch." (Laughs) I always sign 'em and send 'em back.

This is one of the side effects of these interviews.

Yep. Anytime you get a write-up, here comes the mail.

Would you be a ballplayer again?

If I did, I'd be a hitter! (Laughs) As lively as the ball is.

Do you have any regrets from your playing days?

No. Everything I got I owe it to baseball. I'm a little ol' cotton mill boy — never had nothin', never been nowhere. When I got into pro ball, I been in every state in the United States, got to Florida about 20 years, I played in Cuba, Canada, went overseas with the National League in '45 — went to Hawaii, on over to the Philippines. I've been around, just by playin' ball.

* * *

We've mentioned Bill Voiselle's rookie year. How good was it? Just probably one of the best ever. Here are his numbers:

	G	IP	W	L	PCT	BB	SO	H	ERA
1944	43	312.2*	21	16	.568	118	161*	276	3.02

*Led league

That was with a team, the New York Giants, which finished 20 games below .500 and had a 4.29 team ERA. These stats place ol' 96 in some pretty exclusive company.

This phenomenon of rookie 20-game winners occurred on the average of once a year through the dead ball era (19 years, 19 rookie 20-game winners), but in the 70+ seasons since, there have been only 14 more rookies who have won 20. The first table on page 170 lists these 14 chronologically.

Rookies who have pitched 300 innings are listed in the table at bottom of page 170. Voiselle is the *only* live-ball era hurler to do it.

(Sure, Jesse Haines tossed 301.2 innings in 1920, the supposed birth year of the live ball, but in actuality the National League was still in the dead ball era in '20. League home runs were up, but not much, while in the American League they were up a whopping 53.1 percent. The NL caught up in '21, however.)

We switch to a different mode when we consider rookies who led their leagues in strikeouts (see table at bottom of page 171). This is strictly a phenomenon of the live ball era.

To underscore how overpowering a rookie year Bill Voiselle had in 1944, note that he is the *only* man whose name appears in all three tables.

ROOKIE 20-GAME WINNERS SINCE 1920

Year	Pitcher, team	W-L
1929	Wes Ferrell, Cleveland	21-10
1932	Monte Weaver, Washington	22-10
1937	Cliff Melton, New York (NL)	20-9
	Lou Fette, Boston (NL)	20-10
	Jim Turner, Boston (NL)	20-11
1942	Johnny Beazley, St. Louis (NL)	21-6
1944	BILL VOISELLE, New York (NL)	21-16
1947	Larry Jansen, New York (NL)	21-5
1948	Gene Bearden, Cleveland	20-7
1949	Alex Kellner, Philadelphia (AL)	20-12
1953	Harvey Haddix, St. Louis (NL)	20-9
1954	Bob Grim, New York (AL)	20-6
1985	Tom Browning, Cincinnati	20-9

ROOKIES WITH 300 INNINGS PITCHED SINCE 1900

Year	Pitcher, team	IP
1900	Ed Scott, Cincinnati	323.0
1901	Christy Mathewson, New York (NL)	336.0
	Roscoe Miller, Detroit	332.0
	Roy Patterson, Chicago (AL)	312.1
	Jack Harper, St. Louis (NL)	308.2
	Long Tom Hughes, Chicago (NL)	308.1
	Bill Reidy, Milwaukee	301.1
1903	Oscar Jones, Brooklyn	324.1
	Henry Schmidt, Brooklyn	301.0

Year	Pitcher, team	IP
1905	Irv Young, Boston (NL)	378.0
	Orval Overall, Cincinnati	318.0
	Harry McIntyre, Brooklyn	309.0
1906	Vive Lindaman, Boston (NL)	307.1
1908	George McQuillan, Philadelphia (NL)	359.2
	Ed Summers, Detroit	301.0
1909	Al Mattern, Boston (NL)	316.1
1911	Grover C. Alexander, Philadelphia (NL)	367.0
1912	Larry Cheney, Chicago (NL)	303.1
1913	Reb Russell, Chicago (AL)	316.0
1914	Jeff Pfeffer, Brooklyn	315.0
1916	Elmer Myers, Philadelphia (AL)	315.0
1918	Scott Perry, Philadelphia (AL)	332.1
1920	Jesse Haines, St. Louis (NL)	301.2
1944	BILL VOISELLE, New York (NL)	312.2

ROOKIES LEADING THE LEAGUE IN STRIKEOUTS SINCE 1900

Year	Pitcher, team	SO
1922	Dazzy Vance, Brooklyn	134
1925	Lefty Grove, Philadelphia (AL)	116
1932	Dizzy Dean, St. Louis (NL)	191
1943	Allie Reynolds, Cleveland	151
1944	BILL VOISELLE, New York (NL)	161
1955	Herb Score, Cleveland	245
	Sam Jones, Chicago (NL)	198
1957	Jack Sanford, Philadelphia	188
1981	Fernando Valenzuela, Los Angeles	180
1984	Dwight Gooden, New York (NL)	276
	Mark Langston, Seattle	204

WILLIAM SYMMES (BIG BILL, NINETY-SIX) VOISELLE
Born January 29, 1919, Greenwood, SC
Ht. 6'4" Wt. 200 Batted and Threw Right

Year	Team	G	IP	W	L	PCT	H	BB	SO	SHO	ERA
1942	NYN	2	9	0	1	.000	6	4	5	0	2.00
1943		4	31	1	2	.333	18	14	18	0	2.03
1944		43	312.2*	21	16	.568	276	118	161*	1	3.02
1945		41	232.1	14	14	.500	249	97	115	4	4.49
1946		36	178	9	15	.375	171	85	89	2	3.74
1947	NYN	11	42.2	1	4	.200	44	22	20	0	4.64
	BosN	22	131.1	8	7	.533	146	51	59	0	4.32
	Year	33	174	9	11	.450	190	73	79	0	4.40
1948	BosN	37	215.2	13	13	.500	226	90	89	2	3.63
1949		30	169.1	7	8	.467	170	78	63	4	4.04
1950	ChiN	19	51.1	0	4	.000	64	29	25	0	5.79
9 years		245	1373.1	74	84	.468	1370	588	645	13	3.83

*Led league

World Series

Year	Team	G	IP	W	L	PCT	H	BB	SO	SHO	ERA
1948	BosN	2	10.2	0	1	.000	8	2	2	0	2.53

All-Star Game

Year	League	ST	IP	H	R	ER	BB	SO	ERA
1944	National			Selected, did not play					

BURGESS WHITEHEAD

Burgess Whitehead (courtesy of *The National Pastime*).

Gashouse Gang
NL All-Star 1935, 1937

"(The Gashouse Gang) was without doubt the greatest ballclub I ever saw ..."
— Burgess Whitehead

Burgess Whitehead did not look like a ballplayer. He was not very tall and he only weighed about 155 pounds. His health was never especially good. He had next to no power, he didn't hit for a high average, and he didn't walk very often so his on-base percentage wasn't great.

But he didn't strike out, only four per 100 at-bats, and he wielded a superlative glove. He was arguably the best second baseman in the National League and it is probably not a coincidence that he was an integral part of three pennant winners in the mid–1930's. In fact, the Giants went from a soundly-beaten third in 1935 to an easy league championship in 1936 with only one change in their starting eight: the installation of Burgess Whitehead at second base.

Burgess had become the Giants property in December of 1935. They paid dearly for him — starting pitcher Roy Parmelee, reserve first baseman Phil Weintraub, and cash — but the price turned out to be cheap when the results were in. He led the league's second sackers in total chances per game, meaning he had the best range of any of them, and he was second in putouts and assists. Then, in 1937, he led everyone in fielding average, putouts, and double plays and was second in range and assists as the Giants repeated as NL champions.

He essentially retired from baseball after the 1941 season, but returned in 1946 for a final season with the Pirates. He ended his career of nine years with a .266 average and only 138 strikeouts.

He is over 80 now and retired, but he is still a keen observer of his favorite sport. He had the privilege of playing with and against some of the greatest ballplayers in history.

You joined the Cardinals in 1933 and stayed there through 1935, so you were there at the peak of the Gashouse Gang. What are your memories of that team?

Burgess Whitehead: It was without doubt the greatest ball club I ever saw during my 18 years of pro ball. They could do it all — great pitching, powerful offense, and superb defense.

In December of 1935 the Giants gave two players and cash for you. In St. Louis you were nearly an everyday player, but with Pepper Martin, Frank Frisch, and Leo Durocher you didn't have a position. Were you happy with the trade?

The trade was a complete surprise to me as the St. Louis newspapers had quoted Mr. Branch Rickey as having said that the 1936 team would be built around me. As things turned out, I was very happy with the deal since the Giants won pennants in 1936 and 1937.

You were a great fielder with good range. Would you have won a Gold Glove if there had been such an award then?

Absolutely, as Billy Herman of the Cubs and I were considered the two best second basemen in the National League.

What kind of minor league career did you have?

I started pro baseball in 1931 at Columbus, Ohio (Red Birds), an AAA-affiliate of the St. Louis Cardinals, hitting .328 my first year, .316 my second year. I went to the parent club on April 19, 1933.

You were ill in 1938 and missed the entire season. What happened?

I was real frail my whole baseball career, weighing only 155 pounds, and my general health was never too good, especially in hot weather. After having played my first two seasons in New York in practically every game I had a physical breakdown.

You left the Giants in '41 and came back with Pittsburgh in '46. Were you in the service.

Yes, I was in the U.S. Army Air Corps.

Who were the best players you played against?

Carl Hubbell, Dizzy Dean, Van Mungo, Lon Warneke were the best pitchers. Others were Frank Frisch, Pie Traynor, the Waner brothers, Gabby Hartnett, Pee Wee Reese, Babe Ruth.

Who were the best players you played with?

Carl Hubbell, Dizzy Dean, Jesse Haines, Bill Hallahan, Paul Dean, Frank Frisch, Rip Collins, Joe Medwick, Pepper Martin, Jack Rothrock, Bill DeLancey, Bill Terry, Mel Ott, Joe Moore, Dick Bartell.

Who were the best pitchers you saw?

Dizzy Dean was without a doubt the greatest right-hander and Carl Hubbell the greatest left-hander.

What was your biggest thrill or best game?

My biggest thrill as a hitter occurred at Columbus when I got eight hits in nine at-bats in a double-header. Seven were consecutive.

My biggest thrill as a fielder—11 assists at second base which I believe tied the single-game record at that time. This was with the New York Giants in 1937 versus the Boston Braves.

What was your top salary?

$8,500. So you might say I came along in the "dark ages" of baseball insofar as salaries were concerned.

What do you think of today's salaries?

Absolutely ridiculous!

How do today's players compare to the players of your day?

I guess each ballplayer considers his era the tops but I do think in my time the players played a sounder and more stable type of game. Nowadays, it seems, that if a player hits 20 or more home runs and strikes out 150 times he makes $2 million a year. In my day, he'd be in the minor leagues.

What are the biggest or most important changes you've seen in the game in over 60 years?

I never dreamed that the salaries would be as exorbitant as they are today

Burgess Whitehead (courtesy of *The National Pastime*).

nor the ballplayers as assertive toward the owners and managers as they are. I guess in my day we were just chattel. The tidiness of the players is unsightly as are the uniforms with the pants more resembling track pants or sweat pants.

The greatest change is in hitting. If a player hits 20 or more home runs and strikes out 150 times he is acceptable. In other words, the smart part of the game — hit and run, the squeeze, etc. — are no longer emphasized.

Are there any changes you think should be made?

Doubtless, the game of today is what the fans love and, after all, they are the ones to please. As long as they are satisfied, that's par for the course, and why change?

You were a hard man to strike out, only once every 24 at bats. Why were you so tough?

I was not big enough nor strong enough to hit home runs but I was considered a good average hitter as I could put the bat on the ball. In other words, I was a good contact hitter.

What did you do after retirement as an active player?

Two of my brothers and I went into the feed mill and livestock business in Windsor, North Carolina, namely "Whitehead Milling Co." and "Carolina-Virginia Livestock Co." We had some good years and some rugged ones.

Did you save souvenirs from your career?

Yes. Several individual and several team pictures, an autographed All-Star baseball, and an autographed World Series baseball.

Do you receive much fan mail today and do you respond?

I'm over 80 years old now and most people have forgotten about me, I presume. However, I do receive a smattering of fan mail which, out of common courtesy, I do try to answer.

Would you do it again?

Of course I would. I love baseball. It's a grand game.

* * *

As mentioned above, Burgess Whitehead joined the Giants for the 1936 season and was the only significant roster change as the team rose from third in 1935 to first in '36. Burgess remained the second baseman in '37 and the Giants once again won the NL pennant. He had played every game both years but that took its toll and he missed the entire 1938 season. Once again, the only significant change was him, his absence this time, and the club dropped back to third place without him.

The Giants' success in '36 and '37, and lack of same in '35 and '38, can pretty well be traced to Whitehead's defense. In neither '35 nor '38 did New York even have a second baseman. In '35 three men split the position, playing between 48 and 65 games each, while in '38, no fewer than four men saw significant time there. In both years, the defense at the position was only adequate.

But in '36 and '37, when Burgess was *the* second sacker, his defense was arguably the best in baseball. Here is how he stood among NL second basemen in those years.

Year	G	PO	A	E	DP	TC/G	FA
1936	1st	2nd	2nd	1st	3rd	1st	4th
1937	1st	1st	2nd	7th	1st	2nd	1st

He says he feels most fans have forgotten him. No member of the Gashouse Gang will ever be forgotten.

BURGESS URQUHART (WHITEY) WHITEHEAD

Born June 29, 1910, Tarboro, NC, Died November 25, 1993, Windsor, NC
Ht. 5'10½" Wt. 160 Batted and Threw Right

Year	Team	G	AB	R	H	2B	3B	HR	RBI	SB	BA	SA
1933	StLN	12	7	2	2	0	0	0	1	0	.286	.286
1934		100	332	55	92	13	5	1	24	5	.277	.355
1935		107	338	45	89	10	2	0	33	5	.263	.305
1936	NYN	154	632	99	176	31	3	4	47	14	.278	.356
1937		152	574	64	164	15	6	5	52	7	.286	.359
1939		95	335	31	80	6	3	2	24	1	.239	.293
1940		133	568	68	160	9	6	4	36	9	.282	.340
1941		116	403	41	92	15	4	1	23	7	.228	.293
1946	PitN	55	127	10	28	1	2	0	5	3	.220	.260
9 years		924	3316	415	883	100	31	17	245	51	.266	.331

World Series

Year	Team	G	AB	R	H	2B	3B	HR	RBI	SB	BA	SA
1934	StLN	1	0	0	0	0	0	0	0	0	-	-
1936	NYN	6	21	1	1	0	0	0	2	0	.048	.048
1937		5	16	2	4	2	0	0	2	1	.250	.375
3 years		12	37	3	5	2	0	0	2	1	.135	.189

All-Star Game

Year	League	G	AB	R	H	2B	3B	HR	RBI	SB	BA	SA
1935	National	1	0	0	0	0	0	0	0	0	-	-
1937		1	0	0	0	0	0	0	0	0	-	-
2 years		2	0	0	0	0	0	0	0	0	-	-

AL ZARILLA

Al Zarilla (courtesy of *The National Pastime*).

Fournier's Find
AL All-Star 1948

"I was an average major league ballplayer but people said I hustled. Hell, if you can't run to first base you shouldn't be playing."

— Al Zarilla

The 1944 St. Louis Browns won the American League pennant, the only one in the team's history. This is discounted by many because it was a war year and everyone says the rosters were weakened, thus allowing the Brownie victory.

This is said as if the Browns were not involved in the war effort, but it was a war year for them, too. Sure, it's true that they lost no DiMaggios or Williamses or Fellers, but neither did most teams. Gone from the Browns were such players as Walt Judnich, Joe Grace, Al Milnar, John Berardino, George Archie (the war destroyed his major league career), and Fred Sanford (look them up—they were legitimate ballplayers), so they were hurt just as everyone else was. And they still won.

St. Louis had a solid, if unspectacular, team. The pitching staff was led by Nelson Potter (19-7) and Jack Kramer (17-13). The infield was solid and shortstop Vern Stephens led the league in RBIs (109) and was second in home runs. The catching was split between an unlikely pair of rookies: Red Hayworth (Ray's little brother) and Frank Mancuso (Gus's little brother).

And the outfield was somewhat of a four-man rotation: Gene Moore, Milt Byrnes, Mike Kreevich, and second-year man Al Zarilla. Kreevich was the team's only .300 hitter (.301), but Zarilla just missed at .299.

Also, Zarilla, in 288 at bats, was third on the team in home runs and was second in slugging, triples, and RBI percent.

Like most of the members of those '44 Browns, that was Zarilla's only World Series but he remained a solid major leaguer for many more years. In 1948 he was selected for the All-Star Game and finished fourth in the league in batting (.329) and in 1950 he was fifth with .325 (one of three Red Sox in the top five—more on that later).

Al equaled two records along the way. On July 13, 1946, he hit two triples in the fourth inning against the Athletics in Philadelphia. The Browns won, 11–4.

Then on June 8, 1950, in a 29–4 mauling of his former Brownies, he belted four doubles (plus a single). This has gone down as the most lopsided score in history. Other notable Boston performances that day: Walt Dropo, 2 HR, 7 RBI; Bobby Doerr, 3 HR, 6 RBI; Ted Williams, 2 HR, 5 RBI. (The previous day, the Red Sox had trounced St. Louis, 20–4, so for the two games Boston had 49 runs on 51 hits.)

Al is retired now and lives in Honolulu. He really appreciates his fans.

You were 18 when you broke in in 1938. Did you sign with the Browns or did you sign with Batesville (Northeast Arkansas League)?

Al Zarilla: I signed with the Browns. They had a workout camp in Los Angeles and Jack Fournier was the scout and he liked me so he signed me. I went to spring training and if it wasn't for Jack Fournier I'd probably got released because I wasn't that big. He stayed with me and I had a good year (.328).

How well did you know Jack Fournier?

Real well. If it wasn't for him, I'd never have made it. He told me the Browns wanted to release me and he bet the supervisor of scouting that I would hit .300. He won his bet. (Laughs)

Fournier was a heck of a ballplayer himself.

Yeah, the tough old Frenchman.

You had four pretty good years in the minors, but in 1942, with San Antonio in the Texas League, you had a real clunker. What happened?

I had to leave because my daughter was born in California and it broke up my whole year.

In '43 with Toledo (American Association) they couldn't get you out (.373).

That was a very fortunate time to get hot. I think the right fielder for the Browns got hurt so they had to bring me up and I stayed.

In '44 you played for the Browns' only pennant winner.

It was just great. Everybody picked us for last place. We started off and I think we won nine straight ballgames and all at once it dawned on us: We can win this thing!

I was still a young ballplayer, but we had a lot of veterans on the ballclub. It was an honor to get into it because it's a thrill to get into the World Series.

The Series could have gone either way.

That's right. If the ball bounces one way we'd have beat the Cardinals. That would've been a big upset. We woke 'em up after winning the first game.

You spent 1945 in the service.

I enlisted. You see, my number was up. I was in the service the second day after the World Series was over. It worked out good for me. I was married and I had a child and, when I got in, the war was over after one more year.

In '48 you had a terrific year and made the All-Star team.

That was an honor, too. I was a streak hitter and it seems like I started off and I just kept on going. It was just one of those years.

Do you recall the All-Star Game?

Not too much. I was picked because there had to be a Brownie player. I was probably the fourth or fifth outfielder and just played the second half (of the game). (Al took over for starter Pat Mullin in the fifth inning.)

I've been very fortunate. I got in the All-Star Game and I got in the World Series.

You were traded to the Red Sox on May 8, 1949.

It was a shocker but it was a thrill. Here I'm going from the Browns to the Red Sox with Williams, DiMaggio, Bobby Doerr, and that group. And

Vern Stephens, who I roomed with with the Browns, Jack Kramer, and Ellis Kinder. It was a thrill because we had a chance to go in the World Series. I enjoyed the Red Sox.

In those days when you got traded, it was, "Let's go." There was no "I have to see my agent" and like that. As long as you did the job and got paid, that's all that counted.

In 1950, the Red Sox batted .302 for the season and scored 1,027 runs. That's the last time those levels have been reached by a major league team. The lowest average by an everyday player was .294.

I'm hitting about .330 and I'm hitting seventh in the lineup. (Laughs) We scored a lot of runs, but we were short of pitching. We had two good pitchers.

There wasn't the pressure on just one ballplayer. Everybody picked each other up, everybody's having good years, and there was no, "I have to do this." It was teamwork. You didn't say, "He has to play or we're not gonna win."

Williams got hurt and then Billy Goodman batted .350. We had some guys who could swing the bat. (Laughs)

You tied two single game records: two triples in one inning and four doubles in one game.

I remember that one. I should have got five doubles. We were so far ahead and I hit a line drive in the hole and Roy Sievers made a diving catch and it was an out. After the game was over, he said, "I don't know why I made a diving catch. We were behind about 20 runs." (Laughs)

Is there one game you consider to be your best?

It's hard to pick one game.

My biggest thrill was playing in the World Series, playing in the All-Star Game, playing with the Red Sox with Ted Williams, Dom DiMaggio, Bobby Doerr, and that group. And Mr. (Tom) Yawkey, the owner, was such a wonderful person. Outstanding.

But the Browns were great, too, you know. If it wasn't for the Browns, I probably would have never made it.

You were fast. Would you have been a base stealer today?

Probably. It would depend on what type of ballclub I was with. If you're playing with the Browns and we were always in the second division and four or five runs behind, you can't be stealing. Bob Dillinger stole a lot of bases, but that's all. He hit first and I hit second, which helped me, too.

With the Red Sox, everybody swung the bat and there was no use trying to steal. If you get thrown out the next guy might hit a double or triple.

But the game has changed. There's more speed. I probably could have stolen more bases. I wasn't exceptionally fast but I had good instincts.

What did you do after leaving the majors?

After I retired I managed one year in the minor leagues for the Cubs' organization—1956. Then after that I was scouting with the Kansas City ballclub.

I scouted for about four or five years with them, and then Henry Peters, the general manager, went to Cincinnati and I went with him. I scouted with Cincinnati, Philadelphia, Montreal, Baltimore, and Oakland. Then I scouted with the Major League Scouting Bureau.

Did you scout anyone we'd know about?

Diego Segui. Chris Chambliss—I had a lot to do with him. Those were the two main ones.

Segui was a real good pitcher.

He could go nine. The theory now is relief. You have to have a strong bullpen. But if you have four starters like Cleveland had one year—Garcia, Lemon, Feller, and Wynn—you don't need relief pitchers. (Laughs) The game has changed.

Who was the best player you saw?

Probably the best all-around player was Joe DiMaggio. He could do everything so easy and so graceful and everything he did was outstanding. He did it so easy you didn't believe it.

Of course, the outstanding hitter was Ted Williams. There's no doubt about that.

Who was the best pitcher?

You got so many good ones and they were all so different. Of course, Bob Feller—there's no doubt about that—you got Bob Lemon and Newhouser, Early Wynn and Vic Raschi, Reynolds. They had some good pitchers in those days. And Dizzy Trout.

What do you think of Hal Newhouser's election to the Hall of Fame?

Good. You have to go by the record. Don't wait through the years. The record proved what he could do.

How much fan mail do you get?

I average at least two or three a day. It's amazing. Sometimes I wonder where they get these pictures of me. (Laughs)

If somebody asks me to sign something and I think he's sincere, I say yes. But if I think he's a hustler, I'll say no. But what's an autograph? Why say no? It's good to be remembered and if I hadn't been a player nobody would know if I was living. It makes you feel good (to be asked). I enjoy it. That's what you play for.

It's a big business nowadays, but that doesn't bother me. If I get a letter and I feel the writer is sincere about it, I sign the card and send it back to him. There's no problem with that to me.

You should be proud of yourself that you can do things like that. It's a compliment (to be asked). I was very happy and very fortunate to play in the big leagues. I enjoyed playing, it was fun. It's a kid's game.

Al Zarilla (courtesy of *The National Pastime*).

I was an average major league ballplayer but people said I hustled. Hell, if you can't run to first base you shouldn't be playing.

Competition was a little tougher in those days, too. There were 16 teams. I broke in in D-ball and one club — Alexandria — had Virgil Trucks and Hal Newhouser on it. And that was D-ball! (Laughs) But that's what professional sport was then — baseball. Football and basketball weren't much.

When did you move to Hawaii?

I moved here 18 years ago. I love it here. I first came over here for the Scouting Bureau and then they hired me as a coach for the Islanders in the

(Pacific) Coast League. They won the championship here in '75 and '76 and I was the coach for 'em.

I'm retired now. I still help out if I see some prospect here or if somebody wants information.

They have a good baseball program here at the University. Glenn Braggs went to school there. And they love baseball here. I scouted Sid Fernandez in high school here. A lot of scouts brought their radar guns and they said he didn't throw hard enough. I told 'em to take that gun and shove it someplace. I said, "It's what you do when you cross that white line." Some of the pitchers that made the big leagues, like Tommy John or Eddie Lopat, with radar guns they've never have made it. They're the hardest guys in the world to hit.

It's what you do. Nolan Ryan can throw 95–98 miles per hour but he's gifted — he was born that way. But how many pitchers don't throw hard that win? The hardest thing in the world to hit is off-speed pitches and changes. If you can't hit the fastball, you're not gonna hit. You gotta guess at the other stuff and you gotta hit the pitcher's own pitch.

Any regrets from your career?

No. I've been very fortunate. I got to the big leagues and I stayed there a little over ten years. No regrets at all.

Would you go back and do it all again?

You damn betcha! Yes, sirree!

It's a fun game. You're earning money at something you really enjoy doing. You're your own boss. You're actually by yourself when you're playing. Nobody can tell you where to hit or how to field the ball or where to throw. It's a good life, plus you get paid for having fun.

* * *

We talked about two subjects up there that need further discussion: the 1950 Boston Red Sox and Jack Fournier.

First, the 1950 Red Sox.

Once upon a time, a .300-hitting *team* was not unusual. The first time it occurred this century was in 1920, when both the St. Louis Browns (.308) and the Cleveland Indians (.303) did it, aided by whatever went on in the American League that season (some say the ball changed, others say the pitching rules were the cause). That opened the floodgates, and over the next 17 years there were 36 .300-hitting teams, nine in 1930 alone when the New York Giants set the modern record of .319 and the whole National League batted .303. (See table on pages 187–189.)

(Being a purist at heart, we omit from these figures both the Yankees and Tigers of 1936, both of which batted .2998. Close, but no cigar.)

Since 1936, however, only *one* .300 hitting team has appeared: our subject of the moment, the 1950 Red Sox, with a .302 average.

Scoring 1,000 runs is a little different story, however. That wasn't done until 1930, when the Yankees crossed the plate 1,062 times and the Cardinals did it 1,004 times. It's rarely been done, but it was accomplished three more times in the '30s (the last time in 1936), all by the Yankees. But in 1950 the Bosox did it (1,027). (Also see table on pages 187–189.)

How about a .300 average *and* 1,000 runs in the same season. Three times. (Once again, see table on pages 187–189.)

It is interesting to note that of those three teams, none was a World Champion and only one, the 1930 Cardinals, even won a pennant.

So how did the '50 Red Sox accomplish these amazing feats? Table on page 189 shows us the Boston batters with more than 200 plate appearances that year.

And with all this run production, the '50 Red Sox were solid in the field, leading the majors with a .981 fielding average.

With that offense and defense, why then did the 1950 Bosox finish third? Obviously, the pitching wasn't there. The team ERA was 4.88 and the only pitcher with more than 20 innings and an ERA below 4.17 was 18-game winner Mel Parnell (3.81). So, even though they were scoring 6⅔ runs a game, they were giving up 5¼.

The two teams which finished ahead of them, the Yankees and Tigers, each scored less often but also were scored on less often. There's a lesson here somewhere.

Okay, now for our second subject, Jack Fournier.

I have written a book entitled *The Case For: Those Overlooked by the Baseball Hall of Fame* (McFarland, 1992) and Jack Fournier's career is discussed at length in its pages. I would like all of you to buy six or eight copies. You can use them as housewarming gifts, wedding presents, Bar Mitzvahs, door stops, or you can even read one. For that reason (that I want you all to buy several copies), we won't go into great detail here on Fournier, but he was much too good a player not to be covered.

Jacques Frank Fournier was a first baseman, an adequate first baseman but certainly no Elbie Fletcher or Keith Hernandez. He played in the major leagues from 1912 through 1927 (minus 1919) and he was a *hitter*.

Jack first became a professional at the age of 15 and played at various stops around the United States and Canada before joining the Chicago White Sox in 1912, still only 19. He found the pitching unfriendly the next two seasons (.192 and .233), but in 1914 he batted .311 and had the highest home run frequency in the AL.

On August 31 of that season, he became the first and *only* batter of the dead ball era to hit two home runs in one game off of Walter Johnson. (Lou Gehrig is the only other batter to do it, in 1926.) Johnson came in in relief in the eighth and Jack's first homer tied the score. His second won it in the tenth.

The previous day he had gone 3-for-3 with two triples off the Big Train as the Sox had won, 2-to-1.

In 1915 he batted .322 and led the league in slugging (.491). He appeared to be on his way, but the next year he tailed off to .240 and then in 1917 he was back in the minors (Los Angeles, Pacific Coast League).

In 1918 the Yankees bought him as a late-season replacement for Wally Pipp, who was off fighting World War I, and Jack batted .350 in 100 at-bats. This wasn't good enough to unseat the returning Pipp in 1919, so Fournier was sent down again.

Over in the NL, the St. Louis Cardinals weren't much and first base had produced little for them for several years. Branch Rickey bought Fournier and Jack became one of the league's leading sluggers for the next six years. In three seasons with St. Louis he batted .306, .343, and .295, then was dealt to the Brooklyn Dodgers (he didn't want to go and actually threatened to retire), where he hit .351, .334, and .350 from 1923 through 1925. He drove in over 100 runs in each of those three seasons and led the NL in home runs (27) in 1924. The *only* NL batter to finish higher in the Triple Crown categories from 1920 through '25 was Rogers Hornsby.

Fournier's expertise was not limited to the bat. He was an adequate fielder, as pointed out above, but because he was extremely flashy his teams' fans were convinced he was as good as anyone. The Dodger faithful insisted that he was the equal of Bill Terry.

He was regarded as a team leader, was possibly the leading bench jockey of his day (but would not use profanity or vulgarity), and his sense of humor was legendary.

He also took an edge when he could. One time, after a close play at first in which the runner was safe, he told the man that the umpire had called him out. When the runner leaped off the base to confront the ump, Fournier tagged him. Then he *was* out.

His major league career ended after the '27 season (with the Boston Braves). He spent 1928 with Newark (International League), then left the game for a few years. He managed a couple of years in the minors, coached the UCLA team in the mid-'30s, and eventually turned to scouting, working for the Browns and Cubs.

MAJOR LEAGUE TEAMS BATTING .300 AND SCORING 1,000 RUNS SINCE 1900

Year	Team	League	BA	Runs
1920	St. Louis	AL	.308	

Year	Team	League	BA	Runs
	Cleveland	AL	.303	
1921	Detroit	AL	.316	
	St. Louis	NL	.308	
	Cleveland	AL	.3076	
	St. Louis	AL	.304	
	New York	AL	.300	
1922	St. Louis	AL	.313	
	Pittsburgh	NL	.308	
	Detroit	AL	.306	
	New York	NL	.305	
	St. Louis	NL	.301	
1923	Cleveland	AL	.301	
1924	New York	NL	.300	
1925	Pittsburgh	NL	.30733	
	Philadelphia	AL	.30728	
	Washington	AL	.303	
	Detroit	AL	.302	
1927	New York	AL	.307	
	Pittsburgh	NL	.305	
	Philadelphia	AL	.303	
1928	Pittsburgh	NL	.309	
1929	Philadelphia	NL	.309	
	Pittsburgh	NL	.3029	
	Chicago	NL	.3025	
1930	New York	NL	.319	
	Philadelphia	NL	.315	
	ST. LOUIS	NL	.314	1,004
	NEW YORK	NL	.3087	1,062
	Chicago	AL	.3085	
	Brooklyn	NL	.3044	
	Cleveland	AL	.3041	
	Pittsburgh	NL	.303	
	Washington	AL	.302	
1931	New York	AL		1,067
1932	New York	AL		1,002

Year	Team	League	BA	Runs
1934	Detroit	AL	.300	
1936	Cleveland	AL	.304	
	New York	AL		1,065
1950	BOSTON	AL	.302	1,027

1950 BOSTON RED SOX BATTERS

Player	Pos.	AB	R	RBI	BA
Billy Goodman	LF-3B-1B-2B-SS	424	91	68	*.354
Dom DiMaggio	CF	588	*131	70	.328
AL ZARILLA	RF	471	92	74	.325
Walt Dropo	1B	559	101	*144	.322
Ted Williams	LF	334	82	97	.317
Johnny Pesky	3B-SS	490	112	49	.312
Birdie Tebbetts	C	268	33	45	.310
Vern Stephens	SS	628	125	*144	.295
Bobby Doerr	2B	586	103	120	.294
Matt Batts	C	238	27	34	.273

*Led League

ALLEN LEE (ZEKE) ZARILLA

Born May 1, 1919, Los Angeles, CA, Died August 28, 1996, Honolulu, HI
Ht. 5'11" Wt. 180 Batted Left Threw Right

Year	Team	G	AB	R	H	2B	3B	HR	RBI	SB	BA	SA
1943	StLA	70	228	27	58	7	1	2	17	1	.254	.320
1944		100	288	43	86	13	6	6	45	1	.299	.448
1946		125	371	46	96	14	9	4	43	3	.259	.377
1947		127	380	34	85	15	6	3	38	3	.224	.318
1948		144	529	77	174	39	3	12	74	11	.329	.482
1949	StLA	15	56	10	14	1	0	1	6	1	.250	.321
	BosA	124	474	68	133	32	4	9	71	4	.281	.422
	Year	139	530	78	147	33	4	10	77	5	.277	.411
1950	BosA	130	471	92	153	32	10	9	74	2	.325	.493

Year	Team	G	AB	R	H	2B	3B	HR	RBI	SB	BA	SA
1951	ChiA	120	382	56	98	21	2	10	60	2	.257	.401
1952	ChiA	39	99	14	23	4	1	2	7	1	.232	.354
	StLA	48	130	20	31	6	0	1	9	2	.238	.308
	BosA	21	60	9	11	0	1	2	8	2	.183	.317
	Year	106	289	43	65	10	2	5	24	5	.225	.325
1953	BosA	57	67	11	13	2	0	0	4	0	.194	.224
10 years		1120	3535	507	975	186	43	61	456	33	.276	.406

World Series

Year	Team	G	AB	R	H	2B	3B	HR	RBI	SB	BA	SA
1944	StLA	4	10	1	1	0	0	0	1	0	.100	.100

All-Star Game

Year	League	G	AB	R	H	2B	3B	HR	RBI	SB	BA	SA
1948	American	1	2	0	0	0	0	0	0	0	.000	.000

Bibliography

Carter, Craig, ed. *The Complete Baseball Record Book—1990*. St. Louis: *The Sporting News*, 1990.
Charlton, James, ed. *The Baseball Chronology*. New York: Macmillan, 1991.
Honig, Donald. *The All-Star Game*. St. Louis: *The Sporting News*, 1987.
Mercurio, John A. *Chronology of Major League Baseball Records*. New York: Harper and Row, 1989.
Neft, David S., and Richard M. Cohen. *The Sports Encyclopedia: Baseball*, 12th ed. New York: St. Martin's, 1992.
Reichler, Joseph L., revised by Ken Samelson. *The Great All-Time Baseball Record Book*. New York: Macmillan, 1993.
Shatzkin, Mike, ed. *The Ballplayers*. New York: W. Morrow, 1990.
Thorn, John, et al., eds. *Total Baseball*, 2nd ed. New York: Warner, 1991.
Wolff, Rick, editorial director. *The Baseball Encyclopedia*, 8th ed. New York: Macmillan, 1990.

Various editions of the following were frequently referred to:

Baseball Register, published annually by *The Sporting News*.
Who's Who in Baseball, published annually in the '30s, '40s, and '50s by Baseball Magazine Co., New York.

Index

*Numbers in **boldface** refer to pages with photographs.*

Aaron, Henry 66, 106, 111, 149, 154
Abernathy, Ted 12
Abrams, Cal 155, 159
Adams, Ace 3–12, **3**, *7*
Adcock, Joe 100, 106, 143
Alderson, Sandy 140
Alexander, Grover Cleveland 171
Allen, Johnny 18
Alou, Felipe 143
Alston, Walter 167
Amalfitano, Joe 143
Ambler, Wayne 16
Anderson, Sparky 109
Anson, Cap 44
Antonelli, Johnny 130
Aparicio, Luis 66
Appling, Luke **43**, 122, 146
Archie, George 180
Ashburn, Richie 88, 155, 158–159
Aspromonte, Ken 143
Autry, Gene 130, 142
Averill, Earl 139

Baker, Del 93
Banks, Ernie 34
Barr, George 148
Barrett, Red 164, 165, 166
Bartell, Dick 36, 175
Bavasi, Buzzy 134, 155
Bearden, Gene 45, 53, 55, 170
Beazley, Johnny 170
Belanger, Mark 66
Belinsky, Bo 136
Bell, Gary 54
Benswanger, William E. 33, 38

Berardino, John 180
Berra, Yogi 66
Berres, Ray 11
Bickford, Vern 150, 164, 165
Black, Don 14
Black, Joe 106
Blackwell, Ewell 74, 108, 137–138, 150, 168
Blanton, Cy 86
Blasingame, Don 88
Blattner, Buddy 36
Boggs, Wade 142
Bonura, Zeke 82
Boone, Ray 15
Boros, Steve 96
Bottari, Vic 14
Boudreau, Lou 49, 61, 66, 122
Bragan, Bobby 53
Braggs, Glenn 185
Branca, Ralph 110
Brannick, Eddie 8, 82
Bresnahan, Roger 83
Brickhouse, Jack 107
Bridges, Tommy 18, 44
Brock, Lou 88
Brown, Gates 95
Browning, Tom 170
Buhl, Bob 106
Bunning, Jim 57
Burdette, Lew 106
Butler, Brett 88
Byrnes, Milt 180

Camilli, Dolf 34, 40
Campanella, Roy 106

193

Canseco, Jose 141, 142
Carleton, Tex 87
Carter, Gary 97–98
Carty, Rico 88
Case, George 60
Casey, Hugh 146
Cavaretta, Phil 104
Cepeda, Orlando 134, 138
Chambliss, Chris 183
Chance, Dean 135–136, 139, 140
Chandler, Happy 4
Chandler, Spud 63
Chapman, Ben 65
Chapman, Sam 13–21, **13**, **17**
Cheney, Larry 171
Cheso, Reno 25
Church, Bubba 154
Clemens, Roger 125
Clift, Harlond 23–30, **23**, **27**, 63–64
Cobb, Ty 14, 16, 48, 109
Cochrane, Mickey 94
Collins, Rip 175
Conatser, Clint 164, 166
Connors, Chuck 167
Coombs, Bobby 36
Cooper, Mort 78
Cooper, Walker 78
Cottier, Chuck 143
Cox, Billy 106
Cramer, Doc 60
Crandall, Del 106
Critz, Hughie 86
Cronin, Joe 118
Crowder, Alvin 5
Cuccinello, Tony 33–34

Dahlgren, Babe 35
Danning, Harry 82
Dark, Alvin 72, 134, 143, 164
Davenport, Jim 138, 140, 143
Dean, Dizzy 44, 45, 66, 85, 87, 171, 175
Dean, Harry 60
Dean, Paul 175
DeLancey, Bill 175
Demaree, Frank 82
DeWitt, Bill 159
Dickey, Bill 48, 52
Dietrich, Bill 93
Dillinger, Bob 182
DiMaggio, Dom 19–20, 118–120, 181, 182

DiMaggio, Joe 18, 19–20, 27, 28, 64, 66, 67, 98, 109, 117, 118–119, 122, 159–160, 183
DiMaggio, Vince 32
Doby, Larry 15, 64
Doerr, Bobby 180, 181, 182
Donovan, Dick 45, 54
Drago, Dick 45
Dressen, Charlie 5, 94, 96–97
Dropo, Walt 120, 180
Drysdale, Don 44
Duren, Ryne 139
Durocher, Leo 56, 130, 132, 133–134, 174
Dykes, Jimmy **43**, 44, 56

Easter, Luke 15
Eckersley, Dennis 154
Edwards, Bruce 106
Edwards, Hank 166
Egan, Dave 125
Eisenhower, Dwight 66
Ennis, Del 155
Erskine, Carl 74, 106
Etten, Nick 10
Evans, Al 60
Evans, Billy 56

Fain, Ferris 15
Feller, Bob 15, 18, 45, 49, 50, 65, 66, 98, 122–123, 126, 127, 160, 168, 183
Fernandez, Sid 185
Ferrell, Rick 60
Ferrell, Wes 44, 67, 170
Fette, Lou 32, 170
Fletcher, Elbie 31–41, **31**, **35**, 186
Fondy, Dee 166
Ford, Gerald 66
Ford, Whitey 44, 53, 137, 159
Fournier, Jack 180–181, 186–187
Fowler, Art 139
Foxx, Jimmie 27–28
Franco, Julio 88
Francona, Terry 97
Franks, Herman 134
Fregosi, Jim 140, 143
French, Larry 44
Frisch, Frank 45, 83, 146, 174, 175
Furillo, Carl 106, 155

Gallagher, Doug 95
Gallego, Mike 140
Gallico, Paul 45
Garcia, Mike 45, 50, 52, 123, 183
Gearhart, Lloyd 76, 78
Gehrig, Lou 48–49, 153, 157, 186
Gehringer, Charlie 48, 98, 131
Gibson, Kirk 154
Gilbert, Charlie 6
Gilbert, Larry 6
Gilbert, Tookie 6
Gold, Eddie 105
Goliat, Mike 155
Gomez, Lefty 44, 45, 56, 57
Gooden, Dwight 171
Goodman, Billy 146, 182
Gordon, Joe 166
Gordon, Sid 72, 78
Gowdy, Curt 124
Grace, Joe 180
Granger, Wayne 12
Grant, Jim "Mudcat" 45, 54
Grasso, Mickey 60
Greenberg, Hank 32, 93, 98
Griffith, Clark 63, 64
Grim, Bob 170
Grimm, Charlie 44, 56
Groh, Heinie 83
Gromek, Steve 49, 123
Groth, John 98
Grove, Lefty 44, 63, 65, 116, 171

Haas family 140
Hack, Stan 88, 105
Haddix, Harvey 170
Haefner, Mickey 63
Haines, Jesse 44, 45, 169, 170, 171, 175
Hallahan, Bill 175
Haney, Fred 109
Harder, Mel 15, 43–58, **43**, **47**, 123
Harper, Jack 170
Harris, Bucky 56, 65
Harris, Mickey 60
Hartnett, Gabby 83, 154, 175
Hartung, Clint 78
Hassett, Buddy 32, 33, 34
Hatten, Joe 106
Haynes, Joe 60
Hayworth, Ray 180
Hayworth, Red 180

Heath, Jeff 164, 166
Heath, Tommy 25
Henderson, Rickey 142
Herman, Billy 45, 174
Hermanski, Gene 106, 168
Hernandez, Keith 186
Herzog, Whitey 65
Higbe, Kirby 10, 146
Higgins, Pinky 24, 29
Hitchcock, Billy 94
Hodges, Gil 65, 106, 155
Hogue, Bobby 164, 165
Hope, Bob 55
Hopp, Johnny 165
Hornsby, Rogers 66, 187
Hoskins, Dave 53
Hough, Charlie 35
Houtteman, Art 50, 123
Hubbell, Carl 7, 10, 36, 44, 45, 46, 57, 83, 86, 134, 175
Hudson, Sid 59–68, **59**, **62**
Hughes, Leo 26
Hughes, Long Tom 170
Hughes, Tommy 94
Hunter, Billy 65, 151
Hutchinson, Fred 157

Irvin, Monte 154

Jackson, Joe 134
Jackson, Travis 83
Jansen, Elaine 135
Jansen, Larry 127, 131–132, 135, 170
Jeffcoat, George 6
Jensen, Jackie 88
John, Tommy 185
Johnson, Bob 14, 16
Johnson, Walter 49, 65, 186
Jones, Oscar 170
Jones, Sam 136, 171
Jones, Willie 149
Jordan, Buck 32
Judnich, Walt 25, 63, 180
Jurges, Bill 88, 168

Kaline, Al 94
Kampouris, Alex 82
Katalinas, Ed 84, 96

Kazanski, Ted 149
Kellner, Alex 70
Keltner, Ken 24, 28
Kerr, Buddy 72, 78
Kinder, Ellis 118, 182
Kiner, Ralph 35, 104, 149
King, Clyde 151
Klein, Chuck 45, 46
Knoop, Bobby 140
Konstanty, Jim 12, 159
Koufax, Sandy 137
Kramer, Jack 180, 182
Kreevich, Mike 180
Kuenn, Harvey 122
Kuhel, Joe 40, 93

Labine, Clem 132
Lafata, Joe 78
Landis, Kenesaw Mountain 1
Lang, Chip 96
Langston, Mark 171
Lansford, Carney 142
LaPointe, Ralph 158
Lasorda, Tommy 167
Lee, Don 139
Leiber, Hank 82, 85
Lemon, Bob 45, 49, 50, 52, 98, 123, 126, 127, 158, 183
Lemon, Jim 65
Leonard, Dutch 35, 60, 63, 67
Lewis, Buddy 63
Lien, Al 26
Lindaman, Vive 171
Lindstrom, Fred 24, 29
Lipon, Johnny 89
Litwhiler, Danny 71, 72
Lockman, Whitey 76, 132, 134, 143
Loes, Billy 138
Lohrke, Jack "Lucky" 76, 78
Lohrman, Bill 82
Lombardi, Ernie 78, 88, 131, 146
Lopat, Ed 127, 159, 185
Lopez, Al 45, 50, 51, 56
Lucchesi, Frank 65, 151
Lyons, Al 26
Lyons, Ted 44, 49, 56

McBride, Ken 135
McCahan, Bill 15

McCall, Johnny 26
McCarthy, Joe 28, 120
McCormick, Frank 34, 39, 40
McCovey, Willie 130, 138, 140
McDermott, Mickey 120–121
McGaha, Mel **43**
McGinnity, Joe 83
McGraw, John 1, 84
McHale, John 96
McIntyre, Harry 171
Mack, Connie 1, 14, 15, 16, 17, 19
McKechnie, Bill 33, 39, 49
McLain, Denny 96
McLish, Cal 54
McNally, Dave 139
McQuillan, George 171
McQuinn, George 39, 40, 63
Maglie, Sal 108, 132, 135
Mahoney, Neil 123–124
Majeski, Hank 14–15
Maloney, Jim 45
Mancuso, Frank 180
Mancuso, Gus 180
Mann, Earl 147
Marberry, Fred 12
Marciano, Rocky 125
Marichal, Juan 57, 136, 137
Marion, Marty 66
Maris, Roger 154
Marrero, Connie 60, 67
Marshall, Mike 12
Marshall, Willard 69–79, **69**, **73**, 138
Martin, Billy 65
Martin, Pepper 26, 174, 175
Masterson, Walt 60, 63, 67
Mathews, Eddie 24, 29, 106, 146
Mathewson, Christy 83, 170
Mattern, Al 171
Mattingly, Don 142
Mayo, Eddie 82
Mays, Willie 108, 137, 140, 160
Mazeroski, Bill 146, 154
Medwick, Joe 175
Melton, Cliff 7–8, 170
Metkovich, George 15
Michaels, Cass 60
Miksis, Eddie 36, 106
Miles, Dee 14
Miller, Bob 154
Miller, Roscoe 170
Milnar, Al 180

Index

Mize, Johnny 9, 34, 40, 75, 78, 131
Moore, Gene 180
Moore, Joe 81–89, **81**, **85**, 175
Moore, Terry 38
Moran, Billy 139
Moran, Jim 25
Moses, Wally 16, 88
Mossi, Don 45, 50, 123
Mueller, Don 75, 132
Mulcahy, Hugh 117
Mullin, Pat 91–101, **91**, **95**, 181
Mungo, Van 44, 175
Musial, Stan 9, 38, 73, 98, 107–108, 137, 149, 168
Myer, Buddy 60
Myers, Elmer 171

Narleski, Ray 50, 123
Newcombe, Don 106, 132, 150, 154, 155, 158
Newhouser, Hal 45, 50, 98, 183, 184
Newsom, Bobo 26, 60
Nicholson, Bill 88, 168
Nielsen, Milt 15
Niggeling, John 63
Nimitz, Admiral 147
Nixon, Richard 66, 109
Nolan, Gary 45
Norman, Bill 94

O'Dell, Billy 138
O'Neill, Steve 94, 149
Orsino, John 75
Ott, Mel 8–9, 24, 44–45, 46, 71, 82, 165, 175
Overall, Orval 171
Overmire, Stubby 96
Oyler, Ray 96

Pafko, Andy 103–113, **103**, **107**
Page, Joe 118, 121
Palica, Erv 154–155
Parmalee, Roy 87, 174
Parnell, Mel 115–127, **115**, **119**, 186
Passeau, Claude 37
Patterson, Roy 170
Pearson, Albie 139
Peckinpaugh, Roger 48

Peel, Homer 87
Pena, Tony 88
Perez, Pascual 55
Perry, Jim 45, 54
Perry, Ray 131
Perry, Scott 171
Pesky, Johnny 94, 119–120
Peters, Henry 183
Pfeffer, Jeff 171
Pierce, Billy 53, 124
Piniella, Lou 88
Pipp, Wally 187
Poat, Ray 78
Poland, Hugh 146
Porterfield, Bob 67
Potter, Nelson 150, 164, 166, 180

Quilici, Frank 143

Radcliff, Rip 63
Ramos, Pedro 67
Raschi, Vic 98, 127, 183
Reagan, Ronald 109–110
Reese, Pee Wee 106, 155, 158, 175
Reidy, Bill 170
Reiser, Pete 38
Reynolds, Allie 117, 122–123, 171, 183
Reynolds, Bob 142
Rhawn, Bobby 78
Rice, Jim 88
Richards, Paul 71, 72, 139
Rickey, Branch 174, 187
Rickey, Twig (Branch, Jr.) 124
Rigney, Bill 78, 129–143, **129**, **133**
Rigney, Bill, Jr. 141
Rivers, Mickey 88
Rizzuto, Phil 63, 66
Roberts, Robin 108, 126, 127, 154, 155, 159
Robinson, Eddie 36, 60
Robinson, Jackie 73, 106, 108, 137, 138, 155
Rodgers, Bob "Buck" 139, 140, 143
Rodgers, Wilbur "Raw Meat" 61
Roe, Preacher 106, 110, 127
Rolfe, Red 98
Roosevelt, Franklin 87
Rose, Pete 134–135
Rosen, Al 24, 29

Rothrock, Jack 175
Roush, Edd 83
Rozek, Dick 54–55
Ruel, Muddy 49
Ruffing, Red 44
Russell, Reb 171
Ruth, Babe 33, 37, 47, 56, 63, 116, 150, 153, 154, 157, 175
Ryan, Connie 145–152, **145**, **149**
Ryan, Nolan 65, 66, 185

Sain, Johnny 150, 164, 165, 168
Salvo, Manny 82
Samuel, Juan 146
Sandberg, Ryne 66, 70
Sanders, Ray 165
Sanford, Fred 180
Sanford, Jack 138, 171
Sawyer, Eddie 154, 155
Scarborough, Ray 131
Scheffing, Bob 36, 96
Schmidt, Bob 136
Schmidt, Henry 170
Schmidt, Mike 29
Schmitz, Johnny 106
Schoendienst, Red 106, 143
Schumacher, Hal 7
Schuster, Bill 33
Score, Herb 45, 53, 123, 171
Scott, Ed 170
Scott, George 88
Segui, Diego 183
Seminick, Andy 154
Sewell, Rip 34, 154
Shantz, Bobby 98
Shotton, Burt 155
Shoun, Clyde 164
Sievers, Roy 182
Sima, Al 60
Simmons, Curt 154, 159
Singleton, Elmer 26, 60
Sisler, Dick 36, 153–161, **153**, **156**
Sisler, George 157
Sisler, George, Jr. 157
Sister, Dave 157
Sisti, Sibby 146
Skaff, Frank 96
Slaughter, Enos 38, 61, 99
Smith, Mayo 96
Smith, Ozzie 66, 70

Snider, Duke 38, 106, 108, 155
Southworth, Billy 150, 166
Spahn, Warren 74, 106, 126, 127, 147, 150, 164, 165, 166
Speaker, Tris 48
Spence, Stan 15, 60
Spring, Jack 139
Stanky, Eddie 72, 105, 132, 134, 151, 164
Star, Ray 5
Steinbrenner, George 55
Stengel, Casey 34, 51, 121, 125, 149
Stennett, Rennie 149
Stephens, Vern 26, 120, 180, 182
Stewart, Bud 60
Stobbs, Chuck 121
Stock, Milt 105
Stone, Dean 67
Stringer, Lou 26
Summers, Ed 171
Surkont, Max 118
Swift, Bob 96–97

Tannehill, Jesse 116
Tanner, Chuck 140, 143
Taormina, Sal 26
Terry, Bill 7, 8, 32, 45, 46, 82, 83, 86, 175, 187
Terwilliger, Wayne 106
Testa, Nick 136
Thomas, Frank 14
Thomas, Lee 139, 143
Thomas, Valmy 136
Thomson, Bobby 75, 78, 105, 110–111, 132–133, 154, 157
Tornay, Nini 26
Torre, Joe 88
Tovar, Cesar 88
Travis, Cecil 60
Traynor, Pie 45, 46, 175
Treadway, Red 168
Triandos, Gus 71
Trout, Dizzy 98, 183
Trucks, Virgil 98, 184
Truman, Harry 66
Turner, Jim 32, 170

Valenzuela, Fernando 171
Valo, Elmer 94
Vance, Dazzy 44, 45, 171

Index

Vaughan, Arky 35, 45, 61
Veeck, Bill 44, 55
Verban, Emil 109
Vernon, Mickey 60, 64, 65
Vico, George 25
Vincent, Al 71, 92
Voiselle, Bill 163–172, **163**, **167**

Wagner, Leon 139
Waitkus, Eddie 155, 160
Walker, Gee 60, 65
Walker, Rube 106
Wallach, Tim 97
Walters, Bucky 10, 150
Waner, Lloyd 86
Waner, Paul 38, 45, 46, 86
Waner brothers 35, 175
Ward, Arch 1
Warneke, Lon 44, 175
Weaver, Monte 170
Webb, Red 72
Weintraub, Phil 174
West, Max 33–34
Westrum, Wes 132, 134, 143
White, Bill 143
Whitehead, Burgess 82, 173–178, **173**, **176**

Wight, Bill 131
Wilhelm, Hoyt 71
Williams, Davey 146
Williams, Dick 97
Williams, Ted 18, 66, 67, 98, 117, 122, 125, 137, 154, 159, 168, 180, 181, 182, 183
Wilson, Maxie 36
Witek, Mickey 78
Wolff, Roger 63
Wright, Ed 146
Wright, Taffy 146
Wyatt, John 12
Wynn, Early 45, 50, 52–53, 63, 67, 123, 126, 127, 183

Yastrzemski, Carl 122
Yawkey, Tom 182
Yost, Eddie 60, 64
Young, Irv 171
Young, Shorty 167
Youngs, Ross 83
Yvars, Sal 75

Zarilla, Al 179–190, **179**, **184**
Zeller, Jack 93